CW00336631

I THOUGHT IT WAS NORMAL

MICHELE R LEHMAN

© 2022 Michele R Lehman All rights reserved. No part of this publication may be reproduced, distributed, or transmitted in any form or by any means, including photocopying, recording, or other electronic or mechanical methods, without the prior written permission of the publisher, except in the case of brief quotations embodied in critical reviews and certain other noncommercial uses permitted by copyright law. ISBN 978-1-66786-591-1 eBook 978-1-66786-592-8

Deuteronomy 6:4 Hear, Israel. YHVH is our Elohim, YHVH is ONE. 5 And you shall love YHVH your Elohim with all your heart and with all your soul and with all your strength. 6 These words, which I am commanding you today, shall be on your heart. 7 And you shall repeat them diligently to your sons and speak of them when you sit in your house, when you walk on the road, when you lie down, and when you get up. 8 You shall also tie them as a sign to your hand, and they shall be as frontlets on your forehead. 9 You shall also write them on the doorposts of your house and on your gates. NASB

I want to dedicate this book to my Heavenly Father and my Yeshua Messiah for all they have done for me and all they continue to do for me through the Power of The Holy Spirit. Life would not be worth living without them.

Contents

INTRODUCTION

In this book you will notice that I do not use 'proper' English punctuation like quotation 'marks', question 'marks', or exclamation 'marks' as I have learned they are all 'marks' of the beast. These symbols have been around for thousands of years and used in sorcery and witchcraft, etc and have been purposely incorporated into our English language by 'spiritual wickedness in high places' and positions that know exactly what they stand for. You will understand this more as you read chapter 27 on occult symbols.

My mom suggested I explain some of my terms that I use so people will understand what I am talking about. I will try to explain some you may question:

— I prefer to use **Yeshua** versus Jesus because English did not exist in Yeshua's day. If your name is Sue would you want me to continually call you Joyce.

When you look up who 'Jesus' is - you get 'supposedly a prophet', 'supposedly the Son of God', and they even include that the Name of Jesus is sometimes used as a 'curse word'. That is when I stopped using Jesus. I've never heard anyone use Yeshua in swearing.

— **Abba / Ab** is another name in Hebrew and Greek for '**Father**'

— **YHVH** is **Yehovah**. You may know it by Jehovah, but you pronounce the 'J' as a 'Y' in Hebrew. I like to use this because English did not exist back in Yeshua's time and The Father told us what HIS NAME IS. So I prefer to use HIS PROPER NAME. Isaiah 42:8 Literal Standard Version I [am] **YHVH**, this [is] My Name, And I do not give My glory to another, Nor My praise to carved images.

— **Faithful / faithfulness** - 'most' every time you see the word 'Faith' in The Word, substitute it for faithful or faithfulness. In Hebrew the word is 'amanah' and can be translated into English as 'faith, support, firm regulation, agreement'. So Yeshua and His disciples would have lived in the cultural mindset that if you say you have faith in Yeshua then your lifestyle will fully 'support' that claim in every area of your life and that you stand 'firm', not wavering and 'regulating' your life to match that of the Messiah's Life. In Greek the word is 'pistis' and can be translated as 'faith, faithfulness, or fidelity'. Yeshua and His disciples would have understood their cultural mindset to mean that it is not just faith and believing - Again it requires an action on our part. Like 'being faithful' and 'staying faithful' to Your Heavenly Father by following after our perfect example, Yeshua Messiah. James 2:17 Amplified Bible So too, faith, if it does not have works [to back it up], is by itself dead [inoperative and ineffective]. - (dead faith) -

— James 2:14 goes even further to say that this kind of 'dead faith' will not even save you. Amplified Bible What is the benefit, my fellow believers, if someone claims to have faith but has no [good] works [as evidence]. Can that [kind of] faith save him. [No, a mere claim of faith is not sufficient—**genuine faith produces good works.**] Here is a key point I want you to really grasp hold of - 'good works' is always and forever Abba's Righteousness, His Torah, His Law. It is never what we think is right and wrong. Your 'good works' better be duplicating Yeshua's perfect example of keeping YHVH's Ways.

— **Sabbath / Shabbat -** This refers to the 7th day of the week that we are instructed to set apart and keep holy to YHVH. Jews are not the only ones required to keep Shabbat. It is a 'sign' between you and YHVH that you are in Covenant with HIM. YHVH's Sabbath starts Friday night at sunset and ends Saturday night at sunset. If you profess to be a child of YHVH, then you need to prayerfully consider keeping this com-manded day.

— **Torah / Law -teaching -Torah (teaching)-** Torah is YHVH's Instruction Manual. It is His 'Laws'. Some use it to refer to the first 5 books of the bible. I use Torah as the entire WORD where Abba 'Instructs' us in HIS WAYS.

— **Teshuvah** - Hebrew word that means REPENT, STOP what you are doing, and GO BACK ABBA'S WAY. Period.

— **Shama** - Hebrew mindset that means if you 'hear and believe' then you will automatically 'obey'. **'Hear and obey' (Shama)** go together in the Hebrew culture.

— **ONM** - 'One New Man Bible' translation by William J. Morford - takes you back to the Hebrew mindset - even in the New Testament.

— **Gregorian** - the calendar that much of the World goes by, especially the western civilization. Supposedly Instituted by Pope Gregory XIII in 1582. But I have found that Gregori sounds a lot more like Gregorian than the name Gregory. What are Gregori....

— **Gregori** - the fallen angels that left their first estate and mated with humans and taught men all kinds of **symbols**, sorcery, make-up, weapons, how to corrupt YHVH's original creation, etc.

— **Hasatan** - Hebrew for 'the Satan'

— **Holly day** - you may know it as a holiday. But it is anything but a 'holy day'. I say 'holly' day because these are 'pagan days' we are not commanded to celebrate and we attempt to incorporate the Name of our Messiah into these holly days. I use the word 'holly' because pagan/ witches use wood from holly trees and bushes in their sorcery and spells. Does **'Hollywood'** sound familiar..

I pray I covered most of the terms I use and I also pray this will be helpful in navigating through this book.

I am writing this book per Abba Father's Request so I can share with you what Yeshua has taken me through and taught me in order to lead me back to The Heavenly Father. I can honestly quote **Galatians 1:12; For I neither received this from man, nor was I taught it, but *I received it* through a revelation of Yeshua Messiah.**

In 2011 The Heavenly Father sent His Son, Yeshua Messiah, to teach me Who He really is and where I had missed the mark since birth, and who it was I was really following. **Galatians 1:16** takes on a very personal meaning to me as Yeshua took me on a long journey to find the True Messiah and my YHVH:

to reveal His Son in me so that I might preach Him among the Gentiles, I did not rush to consult with flesh and blood.

Please, do not dismiss what I am sharing with you as some nice little story of my life. The Heavenly Father had Yeshua take me through it first so I would be 'better equipped' to help others, so that I could be a preserver of HIS people (Genesis 45:5). Just maybe, you are one of these people, just like me, that Abba is trying to preserve so then you can help turn others from their wrong direction. Read this book as if **'you are the one'** who has been deceived by Hasatan. I did not think I was deceived and had to find out the hard way. Please, pray beforehand everytime you pick this book up to read it, **that Abba will remove all scales from your eyes, break off all witchcraft that would be hindering you from seeing clearly, that all veils be torn in two**, so that you can see clearly what the Holy, Set Apart Spirit is trying to make you see in the Name of Yeshua.

I have been tucked away in hiding since 2011 with very little interaction with no more than a handful of people. The Heavenly Father took me out of the church system and out of my career as a nurse and told me His Son would be my new Teacher and I was given Instructions not to call any pastor and ask them for advice. Abba told me most pastors would not understand what He had to teach me anyways. As a 'watchman on the wall' I will have to admit that most people who are still sitting in a pew waiting on a pastor to interpret the bible for them are still being deceived. Please, do not put this book down in anger with this comment. I want to help you as Yeshua helped me. Matthew 15 warns us: **14 Leave them alone; they are blind guides of blind people. And if a person who is blind, guides _another_ who**

is blind, both will fall into a pit. (a pit that Hasatan/Satan himself has dug for each of us).

You will also notice I say a lot of difficult things, but I pray the Holy Spirit will bear witness with your spirits that I am telling you Truths that have been hidden from us since we've been born. Truths that can literally change your life forever. My prayer for you is that **you will know the Truth, and the Truth will set you free.** John 8:32. Just like it set me free and many others that came to the Truth and who made the decision to make a change in their lives to go back The Father's Ways.

I have watched a lot of lives be completely transformed and even healed by these truths that I am about to share with you, but it is up to each individual person what you do with this knowledge I will share with you. You must make a personal decision to **Teshuvah** (repent and go back The Father's Way) and come out of every false way. I can only warn you. I can not force anyone to '**shama**' (hear **and** obey). This means it is up to you to **obey what you hear** YHVH saying in HIS WORD. I have also had plenty of people walk away and refuse to listen to what I have to say. Especially when I start using bible scripture that they can not refute.

I am not telling you that your life will be a walk in the park with no trouble. Once you make the decision to finally commit to The Father in Yeshua's Name, Hasatan will have a newfound hatred for you to send out his posse after you in his effort to turn you back from these truths. **Do not go back by the way in which you came** (1 Kings 13:17) once you come out of these errors I am going to share with you.

Faith verses faithfulness

One of the first things I want to address is the understanding we have in our English language versus the understanding of how Yeshua and the writers of the Bible would have understood their Hebrew language.

The word faith:

in 'Hebrew' strong's 548 - **Amanah -_support, agreement, firm regulation.** **Definition of Regulation: A principle, rule, or law designed to control or govern conduct.**
In 'Greek' strong's 4102 - **Pistis** - faith, belief, trust, confidence; **fidelity, faithfulness.**
Our 'English' definition and mindset of **Faith**: The assent of the mind to the truth of a proposition or statement for which there is not complete evidence.

Yeshua, who read the Hebrew writings, would have understood **faith** as **'supporting'** YHVH, as being in **'agreement'** with The Father at all times, of having His Life and conduct **'firmly regulated'** to allow Abba's Laws to control and govern everything He did. This is why He never broke a single Commandment of the Father. In Hebrew, a lot of their words require an action on our part. Like the word 'believe'. If we say we believe, then in Hebrew, our life 'requires' **changes** or else we don't really believe.

But in English 'Faith' simply means that my mind believes something without having complete evidence. So when the Bible tells me to have Faith in Yeshua - **I simply believe He is the Son of YHVH** - Even the demons believe that - and shudder James 2:19. Do you really want that demon kind of faith. This is what James is trying to make us see In James 2:18 But someone will say, You have faith and I have deeds. **Show me your faith without deeds,** and **I will show you my faith by my deeds.** 19 You believe that God is one. Good for you. *Even the demons believe that– and shudder.* 20 Oh foolish man, do you want evidence that **faith without deeds is worthless.** ... Now let's go back to James 2:14 if someone says he has faith, but he has no works/deeds - **Can that** (kind of) **faith save him..** James is saying that without a changed lifestyle proving your 'faithfulness' to YHVH then you don't have proper 'faithfulness' and that is not the kind of 'faith' YHVH requires from us because James understands the Hebrew mindset– that if you say you have 'Faithfulness' in Yeshua, the Son of the Living Elohim, then your lifestyle will completely change to match that of your Messiah's lifestyle or you are just kidding yourself - and what you think is 'faith' in your life is 'worthless faith' because it is not producing a changed behavior and 'worthless faith' is not able to save you.

So when you read THE WORD and you come across the word Faith, substitute it for the word 'faithfulness' and watch how it changes the whole verse. Faith and Faithfulness are the same word in the Greek so you are not doing harm or changing the scripture. You are using a better translation into English. This will give you Yeshua's understanding of 'faith' aka 'faithfulness' and it will change the entire meaning of the passage to you. For example let's look at a passage straight from The Word: **For we live by faith, not by sight.** 2 Corinthians 5:7.

So are we just walking and 'believing' that Yeshua died for our sins and that makes us right with the Father now.

Watch what happens if I take it back to the mindset of our Messiah.

— We live by **'our support'** (to YHVH), not by sight.

— We live by **'firm regulations'** (to YHVH), not by sight.

— -We live by **'agreement'** (to YHVH's Ways), not by sight.

— We live by **'faithfulness'** (to YHVH), not by sight.

— We live in **'complete fidelity'** (to YHVH), not by sight.

So when you come across the word Faith now, understand what Yeshua understood. It is not 'believing something with your mind' — it is 'acting' in faithfulness to YHVH, it is supporting YHVH in all you do, it is living in full agreement that you will walk in His Ways only- because His Ways are Righteous, **not ours**. It means we will never cheat on YHVH but walk in complete fidelity to HIM because we have decided to come into HIS Covenant. It means we will 'back' our Heavenly Father in all we do by following Yeshua as our perfect example of life and Godliness by the Power of The Holy Spirit.

I am sharing all of this with you, because, like Paul, I want to encourage you, comfort you, and urge you to walk in a manner worthy of Elohim, who **calls you into 'His own kingdom and glory'** 1 Thessalonians 2:12 .

Let's look at another bible verse and you see which one makes more sense of what the Heavenly Father expects from His child.

-Luke 18:8 ...**when the Son of Man comes, will He find 'faith'** (belief in Yeshua) on the earth

OR

-Luke 18:8...**when the Son of Man comes, will He find 'faithfulness' (children who are following YHVH in all His Ways) on the earth..**

I pray by the end of this book you will have a better idea of how we have been deceived in so many areas of our lives and how we can actually turn back to The Father's Ways and be **FAITHFUL** to HIM ALONE.

CHAPTER 1

My entrance into this World

It all began in the tiny, little town of Van Wert, Ohio. My dad drove up to the Van Wert County Hospital and proceeded to park in the farthest parking spot possible to make my mom walk all the way up to the hospital to insure there would be **no more false alarms**. This was it. I was finally going to make my entrance into this world. But not without a struggle.... and a little quicker than anyone was prepared for. The receptionist at check in was supposedly the nurse also with no apparent doctor on staff at the moment. Upon examining my mom, the receptionist/nurse found she was fully dilated at 10. She put my mom onto a gurney **and sent *my dad* pushing her down the hallway**. Still in the hallway, my mom and dad heard a loud noise coming from my mom and noticed her water broke. But in the process of her water breaking, my feet decided to shoot out all the way to my knees. Still no receptionist /nurse or doctor in sight at this point. Just my dad who was seemingly calm and collected from having grown up on a farm and delivering many farm animals. Here I am squirted out to my knees and my 'good ole farm boy' dad stopped the gurney, walked around to see what was going on, took one look at his baby girl being born, and said, 'It looks just like a pig being born'. Which was actually a very prophetic utterance and a curse over me at the same time as I was making my way into the world. Let's see what the Word says about swine. **Leviticus 11:7 And the pig...... it is unclean to you.** My dad had no idea he had just prophesied that his little baby girl was going to live the beginning of her life so 'unclean, detestable, and abhorrent' in the sight of her Heavenly Father - Like an unclean pig that wollers in the mud. The very animal that even demons desired to inhabit according to **Matthew 8:31-32**. And I have definitely had my fair share of run-ins with demons in my life. Our words are very powerful and parents have a lot of authority to unknowingly place curses over their children. 'The pig being born' would also be indicative of me being bulimic later in life where you 'eat like a pig' then make yourself throw it up. It is a horrible bondage to have in one's life and I was miraculously delivered from it in Yeshua's Mighty Name, Thanks be to my Abba Father.

After rolling the gurney into the room, my dad instructed my mom to hop over onto the delivery bed with both of my lower legs dangling between my mom's legs. Managing the transfer onto the delivery bed, I decided to make a larger grand entrance as the rest of my body shot out -all but my head. 'Well, you got your little girl', my dad said as I began to turn from blue to black. Still no staff members anywhere to be found. Apparently the **umbilical** cord was wrapped around my neck as I was coming out feet first with my head stuck pretty good. The Heavenly Father did say I was going to hit the ground running. Running from hasatan. Running for my life, running from one wind of doctrine to the next. Did you catch the word that resembles **biblical**. Yehovah is very symbolic and Hasatan is a copycat who also uses symbolism to trip us up. Since Satan knew I would be preaching the bible later in life he did everything in his power to cause me to be raised **unbiblical**. He used something that sounded 'biblical' to choke me out. You know the bible verse in **Matthew 13:7 about the cares of this life choking out the Word that was just delivered.** So Hasatan was trying to **choke my life out** before I could be **delivered**. My mom decided to reach down and pull me out herself since my dad was adomit that they wait on some sort of doctor. Praise Yehovah, the receptionist/ nurse finally walked in and told her not to touch me as the doctor walked in right after her. He immediately grabbed me and turned me around in order to pull me out from the dark womb into the light of the delivery room. This was symbolic of what my Heavenly Father would need to do in real life as I would grow up and completely stray from my creator. The Great Physician would grab hold of me, turn me around and bring me out of darkness into His Glorious Light through His son, and my Savior, Yeshua Messiah. I was born **breech** and hasatan has fought ferociously to get me to **breach** my covenant with my Father and my King Yeshua. The very definition of Breach means a *violation or infraction, as of a contract, law, legal obligation, or promise.* He succeeded for a large part of my life. And even after I thought I was following Yehovah, I discovered it was not Yehovah that I was following at all. Everything I was doing was **unbiblical** - Hence **umbilical**. I actually thought it was called '**unbiblical' cord** for a large part of my life because I had heard it mistakenly pronounced as such.

A huge Thank You to my Heavenly Father through my Yeshua for '**delivering**' me.

Allow me to share one more symbolism before I close out this chapter. Around 2011, The Father gave me a vision and showed me as a baby with an **umbilical cord still attached** but it was not attached to anything on the other end but rather hanging in mid 'air'. Where was my sustenance really coming from. I needed to realize I was not being fed by Abba, but instead, my nourishment was coming straight from Hasatan, the prince of the power of the 'air', ...n whom I was walking after according to the course of this world ....in total disobedience. Ephesians 2:2 NASB.

But look at **Ezekiel 16:4 on the day of your birth your cord was not cut, nor were you washed with water for cleansing. You were not rubbed with salt or wrapped in cloths. 5 No one cared enough for you to do even one of these things out of compassion for you. Instead, you were thrown out into the open field, because you were despised on the day of your birth. 6 Then I passed by and saw you wallowing in your blood, and as you lay there in your blood I said to you, 'Live.' There I said to you, 'Live.**

What is man that You think of him, And a son of man that You are concerned about him. Psalm 8:4. Our Heavenly Father is always trying to get our attention and lead us out of our deception and into His Precious Light. What a Mighty YHVH we serve.

I am going to quote from 'The Scripture bible' translation. 'One New Man Bible' also uses the same word in verse 8 for the point I am making. You may be familiar with the very well known verse of **Proverbs 3:5** which is quoted frequently, but what is not quoted frequently is verse 8. **5 Trust Yehovah with all your heart and Lean not on your own understanding. 6 Know Him in all your** ways, and He makes all your paths straight. 7 Do not be wise in your own eyes; Fear Yehovah and turn away from evil. 8 It is healing to your navel, and moistening to your bones. The umbilical cord is attached at the navel. So Abba was warning me to turn away from all my evil deeds which were only wise in my own eyes and not in HIS EYES. Then and only then, could fill me with His Wisdom and **feed** me from the 'The Tree of Life'. Proverbs 3:13 Blessed is a person who finds wisdom, And one who obtains understanding..16 Long life is in her right hand; In her left hand are riches and honor. 17 Her ways are pleasant ways, And all her paths are peace. 18 She is a tree of life to those who take hold of her, And happy are those who hold on to her.

I had so much need of wisdom and understanding of Yehovah's Ways so I could come out of the deception we've all been born into. Hasatan is a deceiver. That's what he does.

I could not figure out why I kept having visions of **ketchup** bottles over and over and hearing, 'we have a lot of **catching up** to do.' I had to 'catch up' from over 40 years that was lost through deception after I realized that all my life I thought I was serving The Heavenly Father and Yeshua but I was actually serving the kingdom of darkness.

CHAPTER 2

I thought it was normal
(for Yehovah to speak to us)

But here I am, now 51, and this is my story. I thought it was normal to hear Yehovah speak to us. I never realized it was not normal until I was 40 years old. No, this topic never came up with my family or a single friend until I was 40 years old.

Let me start out by saying: I am not a writer. Neither do I enjoy writing. But I have put this book off long enough. Abba Father has finally gotten through to me, after setting this book aside for over 2 years now. I repent for this disobedience in the Mighty Name of Yeshua.

If you are reading this book, and you consider yourself a 'Christian' or a 'child of God' - Please, do not put this book down if you feel offended. I say a lot of difficult things. But remember - I was in the same place you may be in right now until Yeshua was sent by the Father to begin waking me up from my slumber. So please, do not give up on this book. Pray and allow The Holy Spirit to lead and guide you into all Truth as He did me. I certainly have not arrived yet as I still have a long way to go. But at least I am now awake, alert, and willing to learn the whole Truth, and nothing but the Truth. I am now 'willing' to Teshuvah (to return to the Ways of Yehovah and be willing to walk away from all sin). Let's look and see how the bible defines sin. **1 John 3:4 says Everyone who practices sin also practices lawlessness; and sin is lawlessness.** But aren't we told that Yeshua came and died so that we could live however we wanted. Aren't we taught that we are not supposed to keep the Law of Yehovah. The Truth is Yeshua came to be our perfect example so we would have a human role model to follow after. He is our demonstration of the entire bible. HE is THE WORD made Flesh. Look how many times Yeshua said 'follow Me'. shouldn't we start taking heed to HIS Words. We are all, every man, doing what is right in our own eyes. The Word says in **Proverbs 14:12 NASB, 'There is a way *which seems* right to a person, But its end is the way of death.'** Abba warns us through His Word in **Romans 10:2...we have a zeal for God, but not in accordance with knowledge. 3 For not knowing about God's righteousness and seeking to establish our own, we did not subject ourselves to the righteousness of God. 4 For Christ is the end of the Law for righteousness to everyone who believes.**

Verse 4 has a horrible translation to change our belief system in order to deceive us.

Here is verse 4 in the 'One New Man' translation: **because the purpose of Torah Teaching is Messiah in order to provide righteousness for everyone who believes.** *Remember the Hebrew mindset where 'belief' would require the action of a changed lifestyle.*

Verse 4 in 'my' translation: The Law did not end with Yeshua. He told us to follow Him. And He only did what the Father said, keeping the Torah perfectly. Here is my translation using the words straight from the strong's concordance:

The Messiah [**was sent for a definite goal**] (<u>**as our influence** *impelling us to action*</u>) in Torah [<u>**to continue far more exceedingly**</u>] in **righteousness where Yehovah is the source or author of His Divine Righteousness to everyone committed to trust in Messiah.**

The Law did not end. Yeshua said that until heaven and earth passed away, not one jot or one tittle would be done away with. Has Heaven or Earth passed away yet.. I actually had to memorize **Matthew 5:17-19** and recite it as a little girl in front of the entire church one day. This was no accident. Abba knew when I grew up that I would also be standing before the body of Messiah preaching this same message some day. **Matthew 5:17 Do not presume that I came to abolish the Law or the Prophets; I did not come to abolish, but to fulfill. 18 For truly I say to you, until heaven and earth pass away, not the smallest letter or stroke of a letter shall pass from the Law, until all is accomplished. 19 Therefore, <u>whoever nullifies one of the least of these commandments, and teaches others *to do* the same, shall be called least in the kingdom of heaven;</u> but whoever keeps and teaches *them,* he shall be called great in the kingdom of heaven.**

Now allow me to explain that verse with My own commentary: Yehovah, through His foreknowledge, knew that men would not keep His Commandments that He would give to mankind to protect them. He knew they would not even have the desire to keep His Divine Laws and they definitely would not have the power to keep them. So He decided before the foundation of the World when the fullness of time should come, that He would send forth His Son, born of a virgin who would raise Yeshua in the Torah Teaching so that Yeshua could show us how it was supposed to be done. Then He would be crucified, rise from the grave, then go to be seated at the Right Hand of The Father so that the Father would send THE PROMISE. The Promise is the Holy Spirit that now gives us the 'will' and 'desire' to keep YHVH's Commandments- then gives us the 'power' to keep them. The Holy Spirit writes YHVH's Commandments on our hearts now. And it is not a New Covenant. The Hebrew language understands it to mean a **re-newed** Covenant. Based on better promises. This time we will be able to keep His Ways because we now have the Promise living inside of us.

And pay close attention to the '2nd writings'. Yes, the 'second writings' instead of the New Testament. Perhaps they call it the 2nd writings because the Apostles rewrote the Old Testament a '2nd' time as they 'rewrote' the Old Testament using their own words to the churches. The 2nd writings are mere letters written to churches rewriting the 1st writings or the 'Old Testament'. We have very poor translations trying to deceive us into departing from YHVH's Divine Laws. Hasatan, of course, is behind this grand scheme in order to get legal rights to us and open up doors to us. Hasatan's whole agenda from all the way back in the Garden of Eden was to make us keep his commandments, meanwhile setting aside Yehovah's commandments.

Check out these passages in the '**First Book of Adam and Eve**' - a book that has been stolen from us and lost through the ages.

This is <u>Yehovah speaking to Adam</u>:

68:5 But it is Satan, your master who did it; **he to whom you have subjected yourself; <u>My Commandment being meanwhile set aside.</u>**

Now this is <u>Hasatan speaking to Adam</u>:

57:7 but now oh Adam **<u>because you fell *you are under my rule* and I am King over you because you have obeyed me</u> and have transgressed against your God.**

<u>whosoever accepts my counsel, falls thereby.</u>

So how much of Hasatan's counsel are we accepting and incorporating into our daily lives. You might be surprised to learn the answer to this. But if you deny the Truth of the matter, then the Truth cannot set you free. Yeshua pretty much told the Pharisees in **John 9:41 that if they could not 'admit' they were blind, then He could not help them.** So we don't do ourselves any favors by lying to ourselves and saying we have no sin in us. Of course we do. We must ask Yeshua to search our hearts, expose our sins to us, so we can Teshuvah and turn back to YHVH's Ways of Righteousness. So be honest and ask yourself who you are being obedient to in every aspect of your life.

The Word says in **Romans 6:16 Do you not know that when you offer yourselves as obedient slaves,**

<u>you are slaves to the one you obey</u>, whether you are slaves to sin leading to death, or to obedience leading to righteousness.

I was a slave to sin leading to death, and had to be awakened to see this. It was a devastating blow to me, but a necessary one in order that I may live. Yeshua did not say for nothing, **'Why do you call me Master, Master and do not do the things that I say.' Luke 6:46.** How can we be sure that we will not be the one who stands before The Messiah one day just to hear the frightening Words, **'I never knew you; DEPART FROM ME, YOU WHO PRACTICE LAWLESSNESS.' Matthew 7:23 [Because sin is lawlessness]**

The Word does warn us that Hasatan is a deceiver. Yeshua also warned us that **we have a fine way of setting aside the commands of God in order to observe our own traditions. Mark 7:9** We had better take careful heed to ALL HIS WORDS and warnings. They are for our own good to lead us into the way of life and turn us away from the way of death and destruction. We had better realize the Word is **talking to us** and not someone else. I thought for sure The Word was not talking about me and was talking about Israel –not even considering that I was now grafted into Israel.

CHAPTER 3

Hypocrite lesson

How the Father finally got my attention: I was going through a really frustrating time with my right hip going out constantly in September 2021. Or should I say in the month of Ethanim according to Yehovah's time. Some would know it by Teshrei. But the Bible uses the Word Ethanim so that is what I prefer to use. Jeremiah was not even joking when he said in **Jeremiah 16:19 that we've inherited nothing but lies.** This statement meant more than I could ever imagine. One day, I had enough. My hip literally went out about every 5 minutes. Of course, it would take some time for it to go back into place so I could walk. Then 5 minutes later it would go out again. With much frustration and tears in my eyes, I went to the Father and asked why Hasatan was allowed to do this to me. I kept hearing 'hypocrite'. I had no idea why Abba would say that to me. I had spent the last 10 years diligently trying to clean up my life to be more like my Yeshua everyday. My desire was to walk in the footsteps of my Yeshua. My perfect example of True life and Godliness. So I kept on seeking my Heavenly Father in the Name of Yeshua to see why I kept hearing only 1 word - 'hypocrite'.

The Father was silent. Then out of nowhere the Holy Spirit began to reveal to me why I was a hypocrite. Abba told me that I am always on zoom classes teaching, 'blessings on obedience and curses on disobedience'. When we are disobedient to Yehovah, it opens the door for hasatan to come at us. He really does come to kill, steal, and destroy us. And don't forget - deceive us. He's a deceiver. That is what he does best. And he's very crafty at it. The bad thing about being deceived is that you have no idea you are deceived. That's the whole idea. You know the bible verse from **Matthew 23:3. Where Yeshua Himself warns the people to do what the teachers of the Law say, but do not do what they do. For they do not practice what they preach.** I was that person in a nutshell. I hear some nuts are hard to crack, but YHVH can crack any nut. Abba continued to tell me I was being a hypocrite because I was not practicing what I preached. I knew Abba had asked me to write a book over 2 years ago. I worked on it from time to time. And those times got farther and farther apart, until I eventually set it aside and the work completely came to a halt on that book. I have so many experiences I feel like the Father is asking me to put into this book, but I believe Abba wants me to first introduce myself and let you know a little bit about me and my life growing up.

CHAPTER 4

The tradition of lying to our children

Let me tell you about a very clear instance in my life when I was about 5 years old. It was xmas time and I was sitting on my dad's lap. He was trying to tell me about Santa Claus. Or what I really call him: 'Satan Claws'. He took the 'n', put it in the middle, **to divide and conquer**, and came up with 'Santa'. I don't think I need to explain the Claws symbolism that he **hooks** us with. He's a deceiver. That's what he does best. And we swallow his deception **'hook'**, line, and sinker.

I would like to say I am not trying to make my dad look bad. He is an awesome, loving, and caring dad. He does everything for me. He was deceived also and was only doing what the entire rest of the world does, trying to keep the lie of Santa going. I was completely guilty of this ridiculous scheme as a mother.

So here I am listening to my dad spew out these lies to his little 5 year old daughter. Why do we, as parents, think it is ok to tell a straight out and out lie to our children about something so dumb. And then we keep the lie going for years until they are old enough to know the truth. And then ask our older children to lie to their siblings who still 'believe'. And then we wonder why they don't trust us after we've lied to them about Satan's Claws, the tooth fairy, the Easter bunny, and YHVH only knows what else we need to repent for. We have opened up so many doors for Hasatan to come in and wreak havoc in our children's lives. And how many times have we forced our tiny little, petrified, crying, and screaming child, who has more sense than we do, to go sit on some man's lap in an oversized bunny costume, just so we can get yet another 'image' of our child to add to the shrine of images we have hanging all throughout our homes. If we, as parents, do not care to tell our children the truth then why should anyone care if Hasatan fills them with lies and leads them from the Truth. **Romans 2:6 warns us that we will be repaid according to our own deeds.** Since we seem to encourage lies being fed to our children, then Abba will allow them to be taught lies. And in return, YHVH's 'children' also will be duped into believing all kinds of lies because we duped our own 'children' into believing all kinds of lies.

I did not hear much of what my dad said, because my Heavenly Father was telling me not to believe these lies. And kept showing me year after year, that the attributes that Satan Claws was said to 'possess', were the same attributes the Son of the Living Yehovah has. Our TRUE 'GIFT' from the sky. Like knowing who is good and bad, knowing everyone's name and where they live, and being able to deliver everyone's gifts all in one night, and he can just so happen to fly through the sky and carry all the gifts in his sled for the entire world. As if they just keep reproducing with each one he takes out to put under the pagan xmas tree that has become an iconic symbol worshiped through the 'holly day' in which we talk to and sing to: **'O Christmas tree, O Christmas tree, how lovely are your branches'**. How do we get so beguiled into singing to a tree. As I got older, I found myself forgetting what the 'reason for the season' was, that I was supposedly celebrating. Was it Yeshua's death or birth. I had totally forgotten because the focus was all on Satan claws. Come to find out, this pagan holly day had nothing to do with our Master and Savior Messiah. It didn't help that I had totally walked away from YHVH through my high school years into early adulthood. I could not even remember how Yeshua fit into this pagan holly day anymore. (witches like to use holly wood in their sorcery). That's why they call it 'Hollywood'. There is a whole lot of witchcraft going on in Hollywood in order to 'program' you a lot easier with all the tv 'programming' so they can put you under their spell, put veils over your eyes so you can't see the truth, then equip us with the spirit of anger if anyone comes against our brainwashed beliefs.

I still remember the daunting question Yeshua would ask me every single year for about 10 years before He finally woke me up about xmas. He would ask me, **'Do you really think I want to share this holiday with Santa Claus'**. I understood He did not want to share this holiday with Santa Claus. But I thought He wanted Santa taken out of the holly day not understanding that Yeshua wanted to be taken out of that pagan holly day. In **my** thinking, I had no idea how we would ever accomplish taking this imposter 'Satan claws' out of this (pagan) holiday at this point. The entire World loves this holly day and wants Santa/ Satan in it - even the 'christians'. The 'World' does not want Yeshua in this holly day at all. But YHVH's children are fighting against HIS Will in order to keep Yeshua in this mixed up festival. We can not have this mixture in our lives if we are to serve YHVH ONLY. We must start praying about every little thing to ensure YHVH is not attempting to remove something, while we are fighting to keep it. It might just be the very thing Abba Father is wanting to get rid of.

As I started feeling bad for following along with the rest of the world, allowing Satan's claws to hook my family too, I started making birthday cakes for Yeshua at xmas time with my children and told them 'Jesus was the reason for the season'.. because I thought He was.. But all the while, I did not get rid of my Mr and Mrs life size Claus that would play secular xmas tunes as they shook their hips back and forth. Looking back, I realize I mixed my Yehsua decorations right along with my santa/satan decorations. A house divided cannot stand. I had a zeal for YHVH but definitely not according to knowledge. And what seemed right in my own eyes was actually the way leading to death and destruction. Father, forgive me in Yeshua's Mighty Name. I was becoming so upset about this imposter Satan/santa Claws and I had no idea how, I alone, would ever be able to remove this imposter from what I thought was Yeshua's birthday.

Allow me to share a tiny experience how YHVH used my youngest son when he was about 6 years old to utter a prophetic word to me, that I did not get at the time. I had taken my 3 children to the mall and as we were walking on the upper level overlooking the center of the mall where Satan was set up to 'lure' the children in to get their 'images' taken with him, my youngest son stops, looks through the balcony, points straight at Santa Claus, and yells really loud the prophetic phrase, **'He's an imposter'**.

What my son meant from a human standpoint was he could tell this person was dressed in a fake costume and was wearing a fake beard. My children were used to a man we hired every year to come to my mother in law's house who claimed to be the real Santa claus. This man was older and had a real beard and a very authentic looking costume. So my youngest son, thinking he knew the real Santa, recognized this strange person in all his fake attire as an imposter. No matter why my son said what he said, Abba orchestrated those words uttered from this 6 year old's mouth to echo a message to not only me, but the entire mall.

A message that should be heard around the World - Santa/Satan is an imposter trying to cause us to follow him in any way he can. If we Truly follow our Messiah we will walk away from the holly day that glorifies Santa/Satan and start following the feast days that we are commanded to keep that brings glory and honor to our Yeshua alone - NO IMPOSTERS WELCOME.

Symbolically, since we lie to our children, to make them believe in an 'imposter' Yeshua under the disguise of Santa Claus, and even pay people to come to our homes and pretend they are Santa. Hasatan is, likewise, able to deceive us adults into believing in an imposter 'baby Savior' named Tammuz and believing it is Yeshua. Who the Greeks call Christos. Tammuz is their Christos, or 'anointed one'. X is a symbol for Nimrod. Nimrod is supposedly Tammuz's father who died and impregnated his wife Semeramis with the ray of the sun. The Illuminati, FreeMasons, secret societies, etc, are all about their 'sun worship' agenda and pushing it off on the entire world deceiving us to come into agreement with the kingdom of darkness. This is why after thousands of years of believing the earth was the center of the universe, they now have us coming into agreement with them that **'everything revolves around the sun'** and that the 'sun' is the 'center of everything'.

Christmas aka xmas is not about Yeshua. I have never read after one bible scholar or thealogin who has said Yeshua was born in what the **Gregori**an calendar calls December. [By the way - did you know the fallen Angels are also called **Gregori**. Just some food for thought.] But Tammuz was born on what we call December 25. Along with a whole bunch of other Greek and Roman gods. Also said to have been born of virgin mothers dating way back before Yeshua was ever born. Allow me to show you where the bible mentions Tammuz. **Ezekiel 8:14-15 NLT 14 He brought me to the north gate of the LORD's Temple, and some women were sitting there, <u>weeping for the god Tammuz.</u> 15 'Have you seen this' he asked. 'But I will show you even more <u>detestable sins</u> than these.'** Notice the fact they are weeping over their 'god' Tammuz and how YHVH considers this 'detestable'. We must come to the place to realize how detestable we have become in the Sight of Almighty YHVH in our daily conduct that we've been deceived into carrying out.

I refuse to throw my Yeshua in the mix with Tammuz and all the other false gods any longer. Yeshua has been proven to have not been born on December 25. So why do we insist on celebrating His Birthday with Tammuz. We are not to copy the way the heathens worship their gods. What part of **Deuteronomy 12:4** do we not understand - [NLT] **Do not worship the LORD your God in the way these pagan peoples worship their gods.** WE HAD BETTER LEARN TO TREMBLE AT YHVH'S WORD - **so that they will not teach you to do all the same detestable practices of theirs which they have done for their gods, by which you would sin against the LORD your God** Deuteronomy 20:18 NASB. Is this where we get the phrase, 'if you can't beat them, join them'. WE MUST ALL TURN AND TESHUVAH FROM ALL COMPROMISE TO YHVH'S WORD. I never want to hear Yeshua tell me to depart from Him because I was lawless. (Matthew 7:23) Instead I want to hear the Words, Well done, good and **faithful** servant. We all must check daily to see who it is we are being faithful to in every facet of life.

CHAPTER 5

I thought it was normal

I had heard my mom talk about a couple of instances where she had encounters with demons so I thought it was normal as I was no stranger when it came to run-ins with demons. I never discussed mine with anyone, so as my children got older, I did not think it strange that they never discussed the supernatural or had any frightening stories of the spirit world they wanted to share either. But as it turns out, none of my children have had these supernatural encounters. This is when I realized it was not normal and not everyone enjoys hearing about them. I have learned to be careful how much I share with family and friends, and even my own children because I am not the same person I once was and I understand they have a really difficult time understanding where I am coming from. Even though I've dealt with the supernatural since I can remember, Yeshua did not start really dealing with me until my children were close to graduating and moving out for college. So my family and friends have not been around me much to gradually get used to the changes I've had to make in my life in order to step out of darkness into YHVH's glorious LIGHT. So when I visit with friends and relatives, I can clearly see how they could see me as fanatical, unhinged, and maybe even crazy. Hasn't that been all of our responses to someone we know that we thought took their Faith to the extreme. We could all probably name someone off the top of our heads that we have thought was crazy or a religious fanatic. I've had to repent for those thoughts now that I understand they were just allowing Abba to remove junk from their lives. I formed opinions and based beliefs about people and mocked things I did not understand.

Because of my knowledge of the spirit world, I've had people ask me if I'm a witch. I am not a witch. Nor do I practice in 'new age' or dabble in the occult. I am no longer part of any denomination, or the latest religious 'movement'. Not even Hebrew or Messianic roots - I strictly follow 'The Word'. Yeshua told us **a house divided cannot stand Mark 3:25 .** So of course Hasatan would deceive us into breaking into thousands of different groups and then he fills us with pride as each person thinks their church is the only church that knows all truth and every other church is just plain wrong.

[According to the Center for the Study of Global Christianity (CSGC) at Gordon-Conwell Theological Seminary, there are approximately 41,000 Christian denominations and organizations in the world today. ... Virtually all other Christian denominations that exist today are the result of a split...]

I repeat - I am not part of the Messianic / Hebrew roots. I live strictly by the Almighty Word of YHVH and my desire is to allow the Holy Spirit to write His Laws on my heart and lead my every move.

I had someone ask me the other day if I went to a church. That person was flabbergasted that I was not a 'member' of some church 'denomination' (**demon nation**) and that I would go against Abba's Word. They spewed out the very well known verse in **NKJV ...not forsaking the assembling of ourselves together, as *is* the manner of some, but exhorting *one another*, and so much the more as you see the Day approaching. Hebrews 10:25.** Let's take a look at what kind of assembling YHVH commands us to observe. Don't forget Yeshua and the disciples were kicked out of the synagogues / 'churches' after a time and had to gather in homes. Let's look at **Leviticus 23:2** Berean Study Bible (BSB) **Speak to the Israelites and say to them, 'These are My appointed feasts, the feasts of the LORD that you are to proclaim as sacred assemblies. ....4 These are the LORD's appointed feasts, the sacred assemblies you are to proclaim at their appointed times...21 On that same day you are to proclaim a sacred assembly, and you must not do any regular work. This is to be a permanent statute wherever you live for the generations to come...**You may be thinking, 'but I'm not Jewish.' If you are a true child of YHVH then you are grafted in and you are to have the same INSTRUCTIONS as YHVH gave the Israelites. When the Israelites were given the Commandments and Laws there was a 'mixed multitude' receiving the Laws - not just Isrealites. Some of the Egyptians exited Egypt along with the Israelites. **Exodus 12:37 The Israelites journeyed from Rameses to Succoth with about 600,000 men on foot, besides women and children. 38 And a mixed multitude also went up with them,** along with great droves of livestock, both flocks and herds. If that is not plain enough then look at **Numbers 15:15 BSB The assembly is to have the same statute both for**

you and for the foreign resident; it is a permanent statute for the generations to come. You and the foreigner shall be the same before the LORD. If this is not clear enough then Pray and have The Father reveal HIS TRUTH to you. As people love to throw these verses in our face, they don't see they are in error by not keeping the TRUE 'ASSEMBLY' that YHVH commands us to keep. Besides that, I assemble everyday, 3 times a day with my parents and Aunt to pray. Plus I hold online meetings every Shabbat to teach THE WORD with people all over the World. And I am doing my best to keep YHVH's yearly Sacred Assemblies - His Feast Days / Moedim. So just like we all do, we speak without understanding. We have a zeal for YHVH but not according to knowledge. We do what is right in our own eyes and we do what we've been programmed to believe and don't know YHVH's Ways of Righteousness.

Back to my previous point: I do not go looking for supernatural events. They follow me everywhere I go. But through it all, I have come to have a better understanding of how it all works with the training Yeshua has taken me through these past 11 years. It has been a long, agonizing, tortuous 11 years to say the least. I fought for my life, my family, my marriage, my health, and the list goes on. As it turns out, I struggle with a spirit of disobedience and rebellion towards The Heavenly Father. What is that old saying: **'I am not what I ought to be, I am not what I want to be, I am not what I hope to be … but still I am not what I once used to be, and by the grace of God I am what I am' – John Newton.**

Hasatan really does come to kill, steal, and destroy us. And he's been trying to kill me the moment I was coming out of my mother's womb.

CHAPTER 6

Shady little Night shades

```
Hasatan has Added paprika,
peppers, tomatoes, ketchup, etc to
everything in order to defile us.
```

Another vivid memory was also at 5 years old. I was sitting inside at my maternal great grandmother's funeral on a bench with my mom. The only thing I can remember is the strong, overwhelming, nauseating smell of tomatoes the entire time. I could not bring myself to eat tomatoes for years after this experience. I never even cared for pizza much into my adult life because of this. But as I got married and had children, I would eat tomatoes from time to time. I even started enjoying pizzas. Then I grew to eat tomatoes and tomato based products frequently.

Somewhere between 30 and 40 I learned that my cholesterol levels were sky high. I was at a very high risk for stroke
and heart attack according to my blood levels. I could not
understand what was going on. I was not overweight. I was
underweight if anything. I was eating healthy (according to
the World's standards), running 1 mile and lifting weights 5
days a week at the gym. Then running about 3 miles in the
evening outside with my husband. How could my cholesterol
be up. Then I saw a commercial one day about tomatoes. Dr
Gundry said, 'If you think this is just a tomato - Think again.'
of Course that caught my attention and made me think back
to my great grandmother's funeral. I always equated them
with death. Knowing how Abba is very symbolic and shows
us things through symbolism, I was determined to get to the
bottom of this tomato thing.

I learned that tomatoes were high in 'lectins' which cause high
cholesterol. How could healthy food cause health problems.
Wait. What a little deceiver. You think it is a vegetable. You
use it as a vegetable. What. It is a fruit. What. It is called
a 'nightshade'. The word, **night**shade, even sounds nefarious. Did you know there are about 2000 night shades that are
deadly poisonous that you should avoid like the plague. Did
you know that tomatoes are poisonous to your dogs. Did you
know these 'night shady' characters called tomatoes are used
for pesticides.

My mom learned a very hard, painful way that these night
shades also cause something called 'Interstitial Cystitis' to
flare up which is incurable. Too long of a story to go into now.
But Abba got my mom's attention. She is now on a tomato
free and nightshade free diet as well as myself. But I must

say the 'incurable' Interstitial Cystitis was healed by YHVH Almighty once my mom repented and decided to Teshuvah. ALL GLORY BE TO YHVH AND THE LAMB FOREVER.

My dad recently realized Abba was dealing with him to eliminate night shades from his diet as well. Remember Hasatan can get us symbolically according to our own sins. Since my dad has cut all **toe-ma-toes** out and repented - the unbearable pain in his 'toes' is healing up. '**Ma**' in Hebrew (strongs 4100) actually can mean 'reason' (used 1 time as **reason** in The Word). Hence, tomatoes were the 'reason' for the 'toes' hurting on both of his feet.

Before I cut them completely out of my diet for good, I will tell you what supernaturally happened that convinced me beyond a shadow of a doubt. I was walking through a parking lot and I had that same, strong, overwhelming, smell of tomatoes. But this time I heard, **'This is the smell of death'**. Needless to say, I am done with those nightshades and no more issues with my high cholesterol levels. Praise YHVH.

By the way - Lectins cut holes into your gut and intestine and allow poop to leak out into your body and wreak havoc. Something called 'leaky gut'. Isn't it just like Hasatan's kingdom to send poop through our bodies.

So why am I messing with the foods you love to eat everyday. Because we are deceived in many areas of our lives and haven't a clue. Hasatan has tainted so much that we are going to need the full out discernment and leading and guiding of the Holy Spirit, now more than ever, to show us what is of The Kingdom of Light and what is of the kingdom of darkness.

Enoch chapter 7 explains about how these fallen Angels, called Gregori, taught man how to defile Abba's creation: **Enoch 7:1.** And all the others together with them took unto themselves wives, and each chose for himself one, and they began to go in unto them and to defile themselves with them, and **they taught them** charms and enchantments, and **the cutting of roots, and made them acquainted with plants.** 2. And they became pregnant, and they bare great giants, whose height was three thousand ells: If nightshades are a species of plant that the fallen angels taught men to produce, then we can see why they cause so many health issues in people and that would explain why over 2000 species of nightshades are deadly poisonous. If these are plants that Hasatan is backing, then we are defiling ourselves by putting them in our bodies which are supposed to be the temple of Almighty Yehovah.

What exactly defiles us. If these so-called veggies are from the kingdom of darkness, then demons have legal right to enter our bodies right along with the veggie. The veggie goes through your body and is eliminated but the demon remains in your body to wreak havoc because it now has the right to. I think it is safe to say that demons inside your body will surely defile you. So as we take a bite of Hasatan's veggie, we are actually taking a bite of a veggie with a demon sitting on it. We've 'swallowed' the veggie deception- **with the demon** -hook, line, and sinker. These demons not only defile us, but they kill us, steal our health, and destroy our bodies, raise our cholesterol, cause Interstitial Cystitis, arthritis, and so much more. So when my dad and mom and even myself decided to Teshuvah and go Abba's way and renounce these veggies from the kingdom of darkness, the demons no longer had right to our bodies and demons had to leave. Both of my parents were healed from INCURABLE health issues and no more problems with my cholesterol levels. How many of us are suffering needlessly because we chalk our illnesses up to being hereditary or a cause of old age and don't ever consider that demons are getting legal rights to us to kill, steal, and destroy us. This is exactly why Hasatan would need to trick us into eating these foods that he created in order to get legal rights to us. He must find ways to open portals to get his demon minions into us and he is not just limited through the foods we eat. He has a myriad of ways he has deceived us in order to gain access to us. The Word promises us Blessings on Obedience and curses on disobedience. Deuteronomy 11 and 28 are good chapters to read for this.

We need a complete renewing of our minds. Our Heavenly Father is not trying to be controlling and tell us what to eat or not eat. He gives us our own free will to decide how we will conduct our lives. But if we want blessings and life and not curses and death, then we need to pay attention to what the Holy Spirit is showing us. Father knows all things and is trying to warn us of the many ways Hasatan is deceiving us, gaining access to us, and by what methods he is using. Obviously Abba is fully aware of what veggies HE created for consumption versus what hasatan has manipulated and changed in order to deceive us and kill us. Abba is only trying to warn us because He wants us to walk in blessings and health. So let's stop looking at it like Yehovah wants to take everything we like and remove it from us to make our lives miserable. Let's start 'seeing' with our spiritual eyes that Yehovah is merely warning and showing us where the actual cause of our miserable lives and poor health is coming from. Just maybe the things we are consuming are coming straight from the kingdom of darkness and were never meant to be suitable for human consumption. Just maybe these very foods are destroying our bodies because they are not what Abba designed for us to eat. And don't forget the demons that accompany these foods from Hasatan's kingdom. So even if the food actually does indeed contain the healthiest vitamins and minerals and antioxidants - remember it also contains demons along with those healthy benefits - any foods that are from the kingdom of darkness put you under a curse for coming into agreement with Hasatan's foods and not YHVH's foods. So the curses will still fall upon you no matter how healthy those foods are found to be. If the Holy Spirit continually points out to you a specific food you are eating, find out why. Do not ignore HIS prompting any longer. It may just be that Father is trying to end some lifelong curses we've been born into because of our ignorance of what is actually from YHVH's kingdom versus the kingdom of darkness. Doesn't YHVH tell us through Hosea **4:6 that His people are destroyed for lack of knowledge.** Doesn't The Word prophecy and warn us in **Isaiah 5:20 NASB Woe to those who call evil good, and good evil; Who substitute darkness for light and light for darkness; Who substitute bitter for sweet and sweet for bitter.** Let's look at Daniel's prayer of repentance to understand what can happen to us when we obey the kingdom of darkness rather than the kingdom of light: **Daniel '9:11' Indeed, all Israel has violated Your Law and turned aside, not obeying Your voice; so the curse has gushed forth on us, along with the oath which is written in the Law of Moses the servant of God, because we have sinned against Him. ...13 Just as it is written in the Law of Moses, all this disaster has come on us; yet we have not sought the favor of the Lord our God by turning from our wrongdoing and giving attention to Your truth. 14 So the Lord has kept the disaster in store and brought it on us; for the Lord our God is righteous with respect to all His deeds which He has done, but we have not obeyed His voice.** Who's voice are we obeying. Abba's or Hasatan's. When Hasatan tricked Eve into eating the forbidden fruit instead of the food Abba had created we can see it had dire consequences. It is no different today. What foods are we eating that are forbidden to us. We just need to be sensitive to the Holy Spirit and allow the Holy Spirit to show us what foods are from Elohim and which foods we need to avoid like the plague - so the plague will not have legal right to come upon us.

Maybe look into eating more cruciferous vegetables. The word cruciferous refers to 'cross-bearing' due to the 4 flower petals on the plant forming a cross. I know in my life, these veggies have lowered my own cholesterol instead of making my cholesterol worse like the nightshades do. They are high in polyphenols which seem to be helpful in lowering cholesterol. All I do know is that if we come out of the kingdom of darkness which leads to death and step into the kingdom of light and start obeying Yehovah and all His Ways, repent and Teshuvah, then all these curses will start becoming null and void over us because Hasatan will lose his access into us. And **the blessing will begin to chase us down and overtake us Deuteronomy 28:2 NKJV**. Who does not want to be overtaken with blessings.

CHAPTER 7

The Good old fashioned prayer position

Yehovah is very symbolic. He causes or allows things to happen in our lives to show us something in our future or to show us what is happening in the world around us. We just have to learn how to be sensitive to The Holy Spirit to show us these truths. They happen to each one of us. We just fail to recognize them when they happen. I tell people when something happens 'out of the ordinary' or repeatedly. Ask the Holy Spirit to begin pointing these instances out to you. It may come in a word or phrase you will hear over and over in a span of 1 day to 1 week. Take it to prayer and ask Abba what He has sent His WORD to show you. Pray for greater discernment. The Heavenly Father wants an intimate relationship with you. He longs to commune with you. **He draws near to us as we draw near to Him. James 4:8 .**

So when I was about 11 years old, I would wake up every single night in the middle of the night in the oddest position.

My knees would be on the floor and my head would be on the bed like I was in the old fashioned '**prayer position**'. This was to symbolize my future life of seeking Yehovah's face in prayer constantly. But before that would happen, it was also symbolic of all the years I thought I was serving Yehovah in Yeshua's Name, but was actually sound asleep even while I prayed. One of my prayers is for Yeshua to teach me even while I sleep. And He does. All the time. Most of the World is sleep walking thinking they are serving Yehovah. I understand this because they are in the same '**position**' as I found myself in when the Father began waking me from my sleep aka hypnosis. The word for 'sleep' in Greek is 'hupnos' hence a spiritual sleep. Sounds like the word hypnosis doesn't it. That is because when we sin and allow Hasatan to come in to deceive us - he puts us under his spell and we become spiritual 'sleep' walkers. Or the '**walking dead**' under Hasatan's hypnosis.

Also be very aware of trends going on around you. Most of the time these are a snare from Hasatan. Look how popular the show was called 'The **Walking Dead**' that actually premiered on Halloween night 2010. No surprise there. We should have all seen Hasatan's web he was spinning right then and there that he caught much of the world in. Most people did not see anything wrong with this atrocity. Look at the name and titles of shows and movies. In **Amos 3:7,** Yehovah tells us through Amos, **that He does nothing unless He reveals His secret plan to His servants the prophets.** Likewise: Yehovah requires Hasatan to do the same thing. That old serpent of old has to tell us what he is plotting. If we partake in it, by purchasing and wearing The Walking Dead t-shirts and paraphernalia, then we come into agreement with his kingdom thus falling right into his plan in the natural. Then he is able to carry out his plan in the spiritual. His plot to kill, steal, deceive, and destroy us and make us like **'dead men walking'** around. The shirt goes over your heart area. Therefore he has access to turn your heart towards other gods and to stop your spiritual heart from beating towards Abba and Yeshua and begin to be a spiritual **'Dead man Walking'**. What is up with all the zombie shows and other garbage that we are allowing these **'programs'** to slowly suck the life right out of us. And we don't even notice. That is all part of deception. You don't even know, that you don't even know. Beware of these **television** shows that **'tell a vision'** of Hasatan's future plans for you. They are created to **'program'** your thoughts and the way you think, feel, and believe. It can suck you in like a black hole -and it does. It is a huge portal for demons to flow through to you. Occult symbols are constantly being displayed over the screen randomly with no rhyme or reason except to give hasatan legal right to send his demons out of the tv portal into you if you come into agreement with his nasty shows and symbols and don't turn the channel. I am quickly coming to the conclusion that it is quite impossible to hold back demons from a tv portal. Even if the show you are watching seems harmless, you must consider all the commercials in between the shows. All designed with the intent to suck you into the kingdom of darkness. Their **'programs'** are specifically designed **to sear your conscience with a hot iron 1 Timothy 4:2 .** So something you would not have watched last year, you find nothing wrong with now. You can no longer point out or catch any cussing or foul scenes you should not be partaking in. And you probably, like much of the world, have no clue as to what symbols represent the kingdom of darkness. We are to never accept the **'mark of the beast'** even if they are 'only' a quick image over a tv screen.

CHAPTER 8

No Sci-fi, this really happened to me

Had this experience not happened to me directly, I would have my suspicions listening to someone else's recount of this anomaly. In the same house and bedroom as the good ole fashion prayer position, I was lying in bed trying to get to sleep. Out of nowhere I see a ½ inch blue light shining through the pitch darkness. It was coming into my bedroom through my closed, sealed, and locked window. It proceeded towards me as I lay there motionless in hopes it would not notice me. As it turns out, it was there just for me. I pulled the covers up as high as I could without blocking my eyes in order to see what was to come of this floating, blue light. I lay helpless and alone in my dark bedroom as my heart felt like it was pounding right out of my chest. The tiny blue light floated right over my forehead and hovered over my forehead for what seemed to be a very long minute. Then it left me and headed down the hallway. I never saw that light again. The strangest part is I never told my parents or anyone about this until I was about

40 years old. As a matter of fact, I went to sleep after that. I was too scared to get up to run to my parent's room. Plus it went down the hallway on the way to my parent's room and I did not want to take any chances of running into that light. I have never quite figured out the symbolism for this instance yet. Because I would definitely have to say this was something 'out of the norm'. I do believe that the Holy Spirit was marking me for His Service one day in the future. I do know that I experienced some very frightening dreams as a little child, of someone I could not see, chasing me and I was hardly able to move or get away from this evil entity. Lots of dreams of me in my scary basement and trying to get up the unfinished steps with that entity after me. The unfinished steps would make it all the more paralyzing as I was just waiting for this invisible entity to grab me through the steps, beside the steps, or through the 2 by 4's of the unfinished stairwell wall, or even grab my feet because I could barely move. I would imagine I have a spiritual target on my back from this light. Because Hasatan seems to be relentless in trying to remove me from the face of this earth. I still do have scary dreams that can be paralyzing. Some I am awake for. As a little girl, I would pray and beg not to have a 'bad, scary dream' at night. I would dread going to bed most nights. Once again, I never spoke to anyone about these matters.

CHAPTER 9

Yeshua took my wheel

I am sure Hasatan could not wait for the day that he would get me alone behind the wheel of a car. I recall my senior year at school. I had all my credits to graduate so I did a work co-op program. I only had to go the first 2 periods of the day, then I could leave for work. My first period worked out really well because I was secretary for my vo-ag teacher. He was very laxed and allowed me to come in whenever I wanted to. I didn't seem to take advantage of this privilege, but if I was running a couple of minutes behind, I did not have to worry about beating the bell as he would allow me to pull around back and enter through the back door, so the office could not see me walk in after the tardy bell.

It was a very frequent occurrence, that he would toss me his car keys and send me out to run some errands and this morning was no different. I was driving his car down a very hilly road with very steep hills, not serving YHVH or Yeshua at all at this point, having drifted very far away through my high school years. Praise YHVH He always remains faithful to us and He knew one day, I would come back to Him with all my heart, soul, mind, and strength. So as I am heading up this very steep hill, full speed ahead, I heard the words, 'you need to pull off into the grass because there is a car coming over this hill in your lane and it will hit you head on.' I thank my YHVH that I did not hesitate to listen. I immediately pulled off into the grass, just in time to see some car almost go airborne over this hill in my lane, far exceeding the speed limit. When I saw and recognized what this car could have done to me, I began to shake in fear. But this did not bring me to Teshuvah and come back to my Heavenly Father even though I knew He had just saved my life that day. This is how stubborn we can be towards our creator. Look at all the miracles Pharaoh would see from Yehovah and yet would not serve Him as his Master.

I will share another instance that Yeshua saved my life, and yet it would be years before I would come to my Father through my Savior. I was driving through some tiny little town with a speed limit of 35 mph. As I approached the end of the speed zone, I began picking up speed and had taken my eyes off the road for what seemed like a split second. As I looked back up I saw a police car sitting on the road right in front of me with its lights turned on parked behind the car he had just pulled over and there was no time to get stopped. I have no idea why they had decided to stop right in the middle of that lane but here they were and here I was about to smash into the back of a cop cruiser. I could not go to the left because there was oncoming traffic. I could not get off to the right because I would run right into the back of the parked cars as well as take out a couple of mailboxes in the process. As I was braced for impact, all of a sudden, Yeshua Himself, or a Holy Guardian Angel sat in my driver's seat over me and took over from there. Supernaturally, my hands were removed from the steering wheel, and my feet were removed from the gas and brake pedals and somehow I watched everything going on all at the same time. I saw the steering wheel going back and forth as I watched my car go left, in between the cop car and squeeze between the oncoming traffic. I could see the gas and brake pedals moving up and down repeatedly as if an invisible foot was actually on them. I watched as my car pulled off the road to the right, into the grass ahead. I was so shaken up over this that all I could do was just sit there trying to breathe and hope I didn't faint. The policeman must have been blinded to this because he did not come and give me a citation for reckless driving or endangerment. He did not even come speak to me about this as if he never saw a thing.

I knew this was the Hand of Almighty YHVH and yet it would be many more years before I would surrender my life over to Him. Even though I would hear the Holy Spirit repeatedly tell me, 'You know if you died right now, you would go straight to hell.' And my thought back was, 'I know'. How ridiculous is that. What is wrong with the human thought process. We have no promise of tomorrow and yet we can not seem to get our act together to give our lives over to our Creator, Savior, redeemer, deliverer, helper, and protector.

Let me share another instance that would occur, almost without fail, for a period of several months every time I would get behind the wheel of a car by myself when it was really dark outside. I had about a 20 minute drive to work when I graduated from nursing school and got a job at a nursing home. I would have to drive both directions in the dark to work my double shifts in order to be there by 6am and drive home about 11pm. I would feel the back of my seat being hit and pushed forward over and over as if someone was sitting behind me pushing and kicking on my seat with their feet. Obviously there was nobody there that I could see with my eyes and it was so creepy that I would end up driving home with my interior lights on the whole way home to try and ease my fear. The spirit of fear and paranoia would come over me to where I was petrified to look into the rearview mirror for fear I would see a demon in the seat behind me. Hasatan had legal right to me as I had unknowingly made him my father in that time period of my life. My very denial to the drawing and calling from my Holy Father left me in the hands of Hasatan as my master.

Then there was the time I had picked up one of my best friends driving my dad's little Ford Ranger Truck instead of my tiny Fiero. The roads seemed to be perfectly clear but as I was talking away, all of a sudden, I was driving across the whole length of the bridge sideways on ice. I was always taught not to panic in these situations so I just kept right on talking as I slowly took my foot off the gas, and at the end of the bridge, the truck straightened out and I just kept on driving like nothing ever happened.

My life could have ended really abruptly many times over, had YHVH not had His Mighty Hand on me during my period of disobedience and rebellion.

CHAPTER 10

A simple camping trip turned into an Exorcist scene

This is how messed up Hasatan had me. I was contemplating marrying a man but wanted to purposely get pregnant out of wedlock before I made my decision because I was completely living in sin and debauchery. I did get pregnant immediately upon trying then immediately had a miscarriage about 4-5 weeks after finding out I was pregnant. I was so devastated. Losing a baby is so emotionally and physically painful. I again proceeded to get pregnant out of wedlock a second time. This is the kind of insane, sinful logic Hasatan will bring you to, when you walk away from YHVH's Ways and begin walking in the kingdom of darkness. **The darkness blinds our eyes [1 John 2:11]** . I ended up getting pregnant and morning sickness set in. It was no normal morning sickness as I just gave Hasatan legal right to me for the simple fact that I was not married and with child. And it was not an immaculate conception either. I was in and out of the hospital non stop because I could not keep anything down. All I could do was dry heave all day long and all night long. It was a life most miserable. Do you know, I actually knew this was a punishment for living in total sin and knew I deserved everything I was going through. It got so bad, they hospitalized me and my Dr was pushing me to have an abortion. He said he did not think I would make it through carrying this baby. I praise my YHVH in Yeshua's Mighty Name that He put inside me a strong desire to carry this baby no matter what the cost. So I stood firm and refused to even consider that abortion was an option. The Dr was forced to send me home with home nursing. They inserted a Picc line and Abba saw to it that I survived this horrific, miserable, and dangerous pregnancy. I recall having this picc line in until I was about 7 months pregnant. I was still extremely nauseated but could manage without the **'use of IV's'** now.

Having been cooped up in a house for months now, my mom thought it would be good for me to get out and get some fresh air. She decided to take me camping and let me enjoy the great outdoors. I do not remember much except laying outside on a fold out chair and feeling so nauseous and miserable and wondering if I would ever feel 'normal' again. But that night is a night I most likely will never forget. My mom also still remembers this night that turned into a scene from the exorcist. I was sharing the bed with my mom. I was actually dreaming that my mom was standing out in the middle of the ocean and she began to sink. She kept sinking deeper and deeper. This was a recurring dream. I hated when I would dream about this. I would wake up so sad as it seemed so real. Later we would learn that we were both sinking deep in sin far from that peaceful shore.

Just like this old hymn:

I was sinking deep in sin,
  Far from the
peaceful shore,
Very deeply stained within,
  Sinking to rise no more;
But the Master of the sea
  Heard my despairing cry,
From the waters lifted me,
  Now safe am I.
chorus
Love lifted me
Love lifted me
When nothing else could help
Love lifted me

Just as my mom went fully underwater in my dream, I was awakened by a very loud static sound coming from the tv. There was nothing on the screen, just the noise of black and white static fuzz turned up full blast. I sat up quickly and attempted to turn the tv off, but to my surprise and dismay, it would not turn off. There was not even a flicker of power loss. If that was not frightening enough, as my mom and I just looked at each other wondering what was going on and what to do, I told my mom I was going to unplug the tv, and if that did not work, we were getting out of there quick, fast, and in a hurry. I reached for the cord and pulled it out of the electrical outlet, and to an even greater dismay, the tv did NOT turn off. I cannot tell you how horrifying this was. I was wondering how you fight against something you cannot see. Yeshua has taught me spiritual warfare and I no longer think this way. But at that point in time, I had no idea how to war against any of this nor was I living the kind of life that I could have had any power, authority, and dominion over the kingdom of darkness. I was full out living for the kingdom of darkness in all my ways. My mom and I both got out of bed and left out of there so fast that I forgot I was pregnant and not feeling well. Nothing else mattered at this point. I thought we were in the middle of the exorcist movie and was not about to stick around to find out what was happening next.

I have also learned that everything that happens to us that is out of the norm happens for a reason to show us something that is coming in our future. Whether it may be the distant future or immediately. So I have learned to seek YHVH in Yeshua's Name when things like this happen. - and this was definitely out of the norm - 'I think they call it paranormal'.

So what is YHVH trying to warn me about in my future because to my knowledge this has not come about yet. I have some ideas what it may mean, but I am not one hundred percent certain on what the Holy Spirit is trying to show me but I will be praying more about this. I even forgot about this instance and was reminded during my endeavor to write this book.

Perhaps this is another reason the Holy Spirit has brought it back to my memory, because I will be seeing, very soon, what events I was warned about that would happen later in life. If I find out before I publish this book, I will try to remember to include the reason for this daunting experience. If you don't see the reason included in this book, please, pray for me and my mom. Because the first go around was awful. Pray that we are well prepared and armored up for the real deal.

CHAPTER 11

Some call it 'Haunted'

Allow me to share some supernatural experiences I had on my job. Since I worked double shifts, I would find myself at the nursing home during a lot of dark hours. Whether early morning or after sunset. I recall one night, I was in a bathroom washing my hands. The bathroom door shut and the soap dish moved down the sink counter and I could not get out of there fast enough. It did not matter how often these things would happen to me, it never made it less scary.

Another time, I had walked all the way down to the very end of the hallway to put some clothes away in a resident's closet. The hallway lights were shut off because all the residents had been put to bed for the night. The facility had fire doors that could be opened all the way, half way, or shut. In case of a fire they were designed to slam shut. So I had the door sitting in the halfway point just enough for me to get behind it to the closet to put clothes away. Keep in mind the only way for the door to move on its own, was to slam shut from the halfway position in the event of a fire. It could not go back towards the wall or closet door unless someone physically pushed this 'heavy' door that way until it latched into the full open position. So as I am standing at the closet hanging up the clothes, I hear the door bang against the closet door, shutting the closet door and pushing me into the closet. I wanted to believe that someone was playing a prank on me and I hurriedly looked around the room to see what prankster was trying to pull a fast one to scare me but both residents were in bed sleeping, and there was nobody else in the room. I immediately got out of there and back into the barley lit hallway to make it back to the area that would be lit up for me. As I made my way up the hallway to the center Hub area, I noticed that all the staff members were all sitting up there quietly doing their charting and minding their own business. We had minimal staff most of the time and it was not difficult to count heads to see everyone was accounted for. Nobody was up out of bed and no human being would have been able to make it all the way back up to the hub area and sit down before me seeing them. It was not a joke. And that door could not have been pushed from the halfway mark to the open position without someone or **'something'** pushing it in that direction- Thus proving even further that this was an entity that could not be seen with the human eye.

So let's talk about a time where it was broad daylight and I was the nurse that day in the hospice room. My hospice patient was just about to die so me and all the other nurses were standing there around the bed to say goodbye. This long time resident did not have any family so we all wanted to say our goodbyes and just be there for her when she took her last breath. I was standing there listening to her heart with the stethoscope to hear when her heart stopped. All of a sudden, I felt a cold breeze go through the room. The door slammed shut. A cross that was hanging on the wall over her head, fell down by her right hand and then slid up the bed towards her head. All the nurses took off out the door leaving me alone with this deceased lady and apparently all the demons that came to carry her spirit off. It was not surprising to me where this lady was headed at the moment of her death. Why can't we, as humans, think logically through the experiences we see others go through. I knew if I died at that moment, I would likewise have gone straight to hell just like she had. If we can see all of this right in front of us, what keeps us from yielding ourselves to our only hope for salvation, Yeshua Messiah, Whom our Heavenly Father sent to save us out of our sin. We are filled with the spirits of stubbornness, blindness, rebellion, deception, and disobedience. The list goes on of all the wicked spirits we are filled with that prevents us from rationalizing logically in order to do the right thing. Satan puts an evil veil over our eyes and blinds us. Notice **veil** is **evil** in the word scramble game and **evil** is the 'complete opposite' of **live**.

On a side note, while I am on the subject of the nursing home, let me tell you how the Holy Spirit never gives up on us. On the **1st day** of every week, what most people call 'Sunday', a church group would come and play praise and worship music in the cafeteria. They would sing all the old hymns my parents grew up on and that I, myself, was very familiar with. Even though I was not serving Yehovah at this time, I was very touched and moved by the music. Here I am 30 years later reminiscing about it. It must have left an indelible impression on my heart. Father, in the Mighty Name of Yeshua, bless all these people that take time out of their busy lives to come and witness to people in these facilities. Residents who do not have any family left and never have a single visitor. Many are just put there to die and completely forgotten about.

Thank You Abba Father for not completely forgetting about me and just letting me die in my sin. All Honor, Glory, and Blessings to my Father and my Master, Yeshua Messiah.

CHAPTER 12

The spirit world manifesting in my home

When my first child was about 4 years old, my husband and I decided to buy a home. After moving into this home, I began to see a little boy that looked like a hologram standing there but when I would look directly at him, the vision would disappear. Not understanding the spirit world at all at this time, I began to think it was what one would consider a 'ghost'. I was so distraught by this spirit I was seeing in this home, that I even called the previous woman of the home to see if a little boy had ever died in this home or even outside on the street in front of this home. She said not that she knew of. The strange part was this vision of this young boy looked just like a little boy I actually knew. For years I did not know what this meant. I would also have recurring dreams that some bad guys would pull up in a black vehicle and take this boy and take off with him in the car. This was so terrifying that when I woke up, it was as if it had really happened. My heart would be pounding in my chest and I would have overwhelming sorrow when I woke up. In the dream, I would be in such a dilemma because I would have my baby girl in my arms, and I knew if I set her down to run after this little boy, That they would take my little girl- So I was never able to run after this little boy to save him. That would just add to the horrible, gut wrenching pain I would feel when I woke up from that traumatic dream. Come to find out, that vision was prophetic, warning me that this little boy I knew in real life would become spiritually dead later down the road. I did nothing about this dream and didn't warn anyone because I did not understand it and I did not even raise my own children in the way they should go. Hasatan comes to kill, steal, and destroy us. I was actually seeing through my dreams that the kingdom of darkness comes and steals our children and the Holy Spirit was warning me that this little boy would end up spiritually dead down the road.

Let me tell you another thing that happened in that same house. My daughter, who is the middle child, was not quite 2 years old. She was quite difficult to put to sleep at night. She wanted to stay up well into the night until about 3 or 4am then she would sleep until about noon the next day. But my oldest son would fall asleep around 8pm and wake up about 7am. Needless to say, I was not getting much sleep, and very tired. I would even try to go sleep in her bed and try to watch her while she stayed up. But that did not work well either. She would have lots of energy and would start bouncing on the bed with me lying there trying to sleep. So I got the idea that I would put up a baby gate. At the time, the only baby gate I had was a temporary one that just tightened inside a doorway. So I put it up. But I did not put it all the way to the ground. Because I wanted to raise it up high enough she would not try to climb it, but low enough she could not crawl under it. And if she did try to climb it, it would fall and wake me up since it was not strong enough to hold any kind of weight. So here I am sleeping in my own bed, in my own bedroom, when I was awakened to my little daughter standing at the foot of my bed. I thought for sure I would be awakened from a baby gate falling from her climbing over it. So I picked her up and carried her back to her room but, to my surprise, the baby gate had not budged from its position- Which was impossible. Not to mention, I really doubted my little girl could have climbed over it to begin with especially wearing her foot length nightgown. How did my daughter get into my bedroom from her bedroom with that baby gate between us. To this day, I believe it was supernatural and that she will operate in the 'gift of Miracles' one day.

Now jump ahead to the next home with my 3rd child. Like I said, my children have witnessed supernatural things, but they do not recall them when I ask them about it. Right after we closed on this home, but before we moved in, I had a dream and saw a demonic looking man coming right through the wall into the family room. I had no idea what that meant for us and proceeded to move into our new home.

My oldest son loved to draw, and would sit out in the kitchen and draw a lot. But once in a while he would come in and tell me there was a man that would stand behind him in the doorway of the basement steps. So I would come out into the kitchen and shut and lock the door to the basement for him.

Somewhere along the way, while we still lived in this house, we were all sitting in the family room when we heard a very loud crash in the kitchen. It sounded just like someone took a big, heavy tray filled with lots of silverware- held it all the way up to the ceiling, and let it drop to the floor. We all got up and took off running to the kitchen to see what had just happened. To our astonishment, there was not one thing out of place. Nothing on the floor. I opened my silverware drawer just to find it was untouched.

Not long after this, my husband and I were laying in bed for the night when the blinds to the right of the bed just opened all the way up. These blinds had a string that had to be pulled in order to raise them and we could see nobody in our room besides us. My husband covered his head with the bedspread as I contemplated what was going on. I was more familiar with the supernatural than my husband was but this was still extremely creepy. Later into the night, as I am sitting on the bed facing my husband, watching him sleep, I was pondering all of these strange occurrences in this home and what I needed to do. I was wondering if I should get hold of some random preacher and have him come to exorcize these demons from our home. As I was sitting there, something grabbed onto my ponytail and just about pulled me off the bed backwards. I had just sat back and done nothing about all these demonic attacks - up until now. But it just got real when they started touching me- and so violently, at that.

There was a time when I was a little girl that I was lying in bed with my hair hanging off the side of the bed and some-thing grabbed my hair and would not let go. This scared me so bad that I do not hang my hair, hand, foot, or anything off the side of the bed to this day. I've had a handful of these frightening, hair grabbing and foot grabbing experiences. But never to the extreme where it felt like I was going to be pulled off the bed backwards and I've never felt that kind of pain that they caused me that night from that hard yank. How do you fight against something you cannot even see. You can't in the natural. And we do not have power, authority, and dominion against the powers of darkness unless we are a True Child of Yehovah. Which is another story. Who is truly a child of Yehovah that has True power and authority over all the power of the enemy. I learned that the hard way too. Let me tell you.

I forget who I called, but they told me to just grab some oil in my home, and go through my home anointing the doorways with oil. I did as I was instructed and this was actually the end of all the demonic activity *at this home*. This was also before the time frame that YHVH instructed me not to call any pastors for advice. It was only by YHVH's Grace that He allowed this to work for me. I did not have the power and authority at this time to cast out any demons since I was not serving YHVH at all like I should have been. I was simply 'playing church' and I was definitely not all '**in**' with all my heart, soul, mind, and strength. I 'confessed HIM with my lips' but the rest of my entire being was devoted to the kingdom of darkness and I was completely unaware. I was about to be taught some painful lessons. (hence the pain I felt from Hasatan yanking my pony tail) Hasatan was about to come back for his dues and he was going to yank me around until I realized that I had made him my master. The 'blind' being pulled 'up' by some 'spirit' was because I was walking around '**spiritually blind**' and needed to be *woken* 'up'. I needed the **blind**ers 'lifted' so I could see clearly what was going on in this world of deception.

CHAPTER 13

I broke a vow

In my mid 30's, I had made a vow to YHVH that I would not buy anything for a period of time. I was seeking Yehovah for something, but I cannot recall what that something was. I loved to shop and buy stuff, so I thought giving up shopping for a time would be a good 'deal' to make with YHVH in order to get what I was asking for in return. Yes, I realize now this is not how we operate with Almighty Yehovah.

I did not read the Word very closely for myself and had been taught growing up, you can ask Abba for something if you, in turn, will give Him something on your end. So this is what I was doing. 'Making a deal' with Yehovah.

I was vaguely familiar with the bible verse in **Deuteronomy 23:21 NASB 'When you make a vow to the LORD your God, you shall not delay to pay it, for the LORD your God will certainly require it of you, and it will be a sin for you.'** Of course there are several bible verses about making vows. Here is one in **Ecclesiastes 5:5 NASB It is better that you not vow, than vow and not pay.**

And let's not forget what our Yeshua Messiah warned us in **Matthew 5:33 'Again, you have heard that the ancients were told, 'YOU SHALL NOT MAKE FALSE VOWS, BUT SHALL FULFILL YOUR VOWS TO THE LORD.' 34 But I say to you, <u>take no oath at all,</u> neither by heaven, for it is the throne of God, 35 nor by the earth, for it is the footstool of His feet, nor by Jerusalem, for it is THE CITY OF THE GREAT KING. 36 Nor shall you take an oath by your head, for you cannot make a single hair white or black. 37 But make sure your statement is, 'Yes, yes' or 'No, no'; <u>anything beyond these is of evil origin.</u>**

I personally believe Yeshua got this from the book called **'First Book of Adam and Eve'**. Here is a little clip from that book starting in chapter 70:12. I call it 'The old handshake agreement'. Looks like it was taught by the ole deceiver himself. That is why Yeshua can say that if you make a vow, it originated from the evil one.

'First Book of Adam and Eve'

By Rutherford H. Platt

THE OLD HANDSHAKE AGREEMENT

70:12 and <u>**Satan said to him (Adam)**</u> swear and promise me that you will receive it. Then **<u>Adam said I do not know how to swear and promise</u>** and Satan said to him hold out your hand and put it inside my hand. then Adam held out his hand and put it into Satan's hand when Satan said to him say now 'so true as God is living rational and speaking who raised the stars in heaven and established the dry ground on the waters and has created me out of the four elements and out of the dust the earth **<u>I will not break my promise nor renounce my word'. and Adam swore the thus.</u>**

Can you see why Yeshua could have been referring to this book and passage to 'attribute the origin of a vow from the evil one'. Look at what **Proverbs 22:26** says **Do not be one of those who shakes hands in a pledge...**

At any rate, I had joined a coed softball team with my husband without owning a pair of cleats. I played the outfield, and found myself slipping and sliding all over the outfield running after these balls. I never knew grass could be so slippery. I did not know how I was going to go through another softball game in my tennis shoes. I am sure that grass probably is not that slippery. Hasatan was making it extra slippery to tempt me to buy some cleats for myself before the next game. I used to run in the grass all the time with my friends playing tag and what not. I never recall slippery grass. I think we all know how the story went. I was deceived into justifying going out and purchasing some cleats for the next game, knowing full well my vow had not ended yet. I thought for sure the 'Good Lord' would understand and would not want me injuring myself out there in the outfield.

This is not the Mind of YHVH at all. We are to uphold our word and if we make a vow, we are to keep it. Yeshua knows what is in man. That is why He warns us to not make any vows so we won't sin when we break it.

I was actually so relieved to have these cleats as I was standing in the outfield waiting for a ball that I could actually run after without sliding all over the place. Sin always seems fine for a moment. But woe to us when Hasatan comes back for his dues. As I stood there in the outfield, my right foot began hurting and by the time I got home, I could not take those cleats off fast enough. My two middle toes were red, hot, extremely enlarged and swollen, and incredibly painful. I have had gout before and this hurt like gout, but it was not gout this time. I knew the moment I saw my toes, that I had sinned and I deserved this punishment.

I had to see an arthritis specialist for rheumatoid arthritis and was diagnosed with **Ankylosing Spondylitis (AS)**. Let me remind you of the quote by R Zaccharias: 'Sin will take you farther than you want to go, cost you more than you want to pay, and keep you longer than you want to stay'. This disease is very painful, deforming, and can be very debilitating during flare ups. And it is not just confined to your toes. Because of this **AS** I have had my knees fill up with fluid on multiple occasions - so much that I could barely walk or bend my leg. I have had something called iritis flare up in both of my eyes on multiple occasions which is excruciatingly painful and debilitating. I had it in both eyes at the same time once which made it impossible to see. Everyone was just a blur. I could not even see someone's face to see who was who and until they spoke I could not tell who was in front of me. Obviously I could not drive at all. Hasatan had the legal right to blind me because I was walking around spiritually blind. The slightest bit of light sends horrible pain through your head. I could not even look at the time on my alarm clock because just that little bit of light from my clock was unbearably painful. I was now on what was supposed to be a 'lifelong' medicine to control this horrific arthritis. Which, come to find out, was very dangerous and you could just fall over dead with this medication can cause sudden death. Abba has since allowed me to go off this medication and actually stop seeing this doctor. Once I started learning YHVH's Ways, repenting, and deciding to Teshuvah back to Abba's Ways, My Great 'I AM' has been very gracious to me.

Nothing good ever came out of this disease. My car window was even busted out and my purse stolen while I was inside this Dr's office being seen for this awful punishment of a disease. Not to mention, I hated writing out a check to this doctor as right in the middle of my account number were 3 6's. This 'mark of the beast' was a constant reminder of my sin towards my Heavenly Father in breaking my vow to ALMIGHTY YHVH.

I used to have very pretty toes in perfect alignment. But once the swelling went down, it left my 2 middle toes deformed with the one called a 'hammer toe'. They are not at all pretty any longer. I am actually 'pretty' embarrassed of them. I can say breaking my vow and buying those cleats was not at all worth the misery I have had to endure since the very day I transgressed my vow to Abba. Not to mention, I look like a freak of nature with my right eye being fully dilated now from my last bout of iritis. For the last ten years, I have been walking around with one black eye and one blue eye. (Hasatan loves to beat us up until we are black and blue).. It is so ugly, that people seem not to be able to help themselves with the questions and comments. Let me remind you why our punishment is much more severe than our sin. YHVH said He needs His children to see how much HE hates sin and wants us to loath sin as HE loathes sin. This technique surely does work. I am a little slow getting rid of my rebellious and disobedient spirit -and I am by no means perfect or even close to it but I've grown to hate sin and have learned to loathe myself when I do sin. I have learned to be quicker to repent and Teshuvah which in turn lessens our punishments. **Leviticus 26** starting at verse 14 is a good chapter of how The Father attempts to use punishment to break down our stubborn pride and start walking His Ways.

Allow me to share another excerpt from the **'First Book of Adam and Eve'.** I knew exactly where Adam was coming from when he asked Yehovah this question, that I myself had asked The Father several times over.

'First Book of Adam and Eve'

By Rutherford H. Platt

37:5 We transgressed against you 1 hour and all these trials and sorrows have come over us until this day.

-in chapter 59 verse 8 Adam asks YHVH why the severe punishment compared to his sin:

59:8 then Adam cried before the Lord and said oh Lord because I transgressed a little you have severely punished me and returned for it.

Sounds like Luke understood this concept. Check out Luke 6:38 Give, and it will be given to you. A good measure, pressed down, shaken together, and running over will be poured into your lap. For with the measure you use, it will be measured back to you.

The Word of YHVH agrees with this concept that we get back more than we dished out. Whether it be good or bad.

We could all do ourselves a little favor and memorize **Romans 6:16: Do you not know that when you offer yourselves as obedient slaves, you are slaves to the one you obey,** whether you are slaves to sin leading to death, or to obedience leading to righteousness.

Check out what Hasatan told Adam after he sinned:

'First Book of Adam and Eve'

By Rutherford H. Platt

57:2 then **Satan answered** and said to Adam it is I who hid myself within the serpent and who spoke to Eve and **who enticed her until she obeyed my command** I am he who sent her **using my deceitful speech to deceive** you until you both ate of the fruit of the tree **and abandoned the command of God.**

57:7 but now oh Adam because you fell you are under my rule and I am King over you because you have obeyed me and have transgressed against your God. neither will there be any deliverance from my hands until the day promised you by your God.

Here is what YHVH has to say to help us understand we had better be careful who we make our ruler. WE had better start paying attention to whose commands we are obeying.

68:5 (Yehovah says to Adam) -but it is Satan your master who did it. he to whom you have subjected yourself.

my commandment being meanwhile set aside

With that being said, you had better take a real hard look in the Word to find where Yehovah commands us to keep Xmas, the bunny rabbit holly day, Valentines Day, etc. YOU WILL NOT FIND ANY OF THESE. These are all a trick straight from the pit of hell in order to make Hasatan our ruler. By keeping the days of Satan, we lay aside the Feast Days that Yehovah commands us to keep yearly as our Moedim. We are commanded not to forsake the 'assembling' together. We are to 'assemble' at YHVH's Feasts and not Hasatan's festivities.

We are commanded By YHVH to keep Shabbat and all YHVH's Feast Days. We are to keep Passover and not Easter, which is an English word for Ishtar. They are not even celebrated at the same time most years. So which ones are you keeping.. Whom have you made your ruler. I had to learn this the hard way and Teshuvah. Hasatan almost killed me while being my ruler. He is one hard taskmaster and the wages of sin is definitely death. A long, hard, agonizing path to death and destruction. I know this all too well.

We had better find out who our 'master' really is.

I do not remember what I ever did with those cleats but I no longer have them. I can't even remember playing ball after that because it was way too painful for months to even walk.

CHAPTER 14

My Great Awakening with
my very first visions

In 2011 Yeshua began to awaken me from my spiritual slumber. Abba, being very symbolic, had His WORD awaken me out of my physical sleep and asked me to go to the closet for Him to show me some things. He showed me my 3rd vision after giving me my very first two visions the day before while sitting at the kitchen table. I had never had a vision to this point, and it caused me to enter into about 3 months of very thick darkness, oppression and confusion because I did not know what was happening to me. I thought for sure that Hasatan was tricking me and I would die and go to hell. Especially since my 3rd vision was of a huge, black python coming out of a pastor's mouth and it grew tentacles that went out into the congregation and began wrapping around everyone's ankles. I did not want to tell anyone for fear they would think I was losing my mind and I felt all alone with nobody to turn to. After about 3 to 4 months I recall one of the first people I told was my maternal grandma. I thought if anyone understood and had my back, it would be her. She talked about the 'Good Lord' all the time. To my dismay, her response to what I had confided to her was, 'be very careful, satan is a deceiver'. This was not at all what I was expecting her to say, and I am super glad I did not approach her at the beginning when I was unclear as to what was going on. I could have possibly missed out on the opportunity of allowing Abba to work with me and **show me great and mighty things which I did not now know or understand** Jeremiah 33:3.

I learned He gives me visions to warn me when I am going in the wrong direction to show me when I need to repent and Teshuvah. He shows me private matters going on in people's lives so I know how to pray for them. A lot of times I have visions that I do not understand until He makes the meaning known to me. Yeshua, through the Power of the Holy Spirit, is Truly the Greatest Teacher anyone could ever hope to have.

CHAPTER 15

A Prophecy by Stanley Frodsham

I would like to share a link to a prophecy from a man named Stanely Frodsham. This prophecy was given to Stanley Frodsham in 1965. But around 2011, Abba made sure I found it. This bore witness with my spirit, that this prophecy was directly from Yehovah given to Yeshua to give to Stanley Frodsham back in 1965. So as we jump forward in my life to around 2011, Abba now had my attention. I thought I was 100 percent dedicated to my Heavenly Father in Yeshua's Name. But He would need to take me through a series of events to show me I was way off Target. I also needed to go through some bootcamp training with Yeshua, to be prepared for the upcoming days ahead. Please, take heed to this prophecy, as I am fully convinced that it was given for the time we are now entering into. Abba desires to prepare His True Bride - without spot or wrinkle. I was completely unaware that I was actually an imposter bride who had gone a whoring after everything but Yehovah. My prayer is that more people will be awakened to the deceptions that have been indoctrinated into us. **Jeremiah 16:19** warns us we have **inherited nothing but falsehood, futility, and things of no profit.**

You must understand that at the time of my 'great awakening' my entire life was devoted to Yeshua and Abba. I was a praise and worship leader at my church as well as the head treasurer. Then I became a full time youth pastor. Everything I did revolved around my Abba and Yeshua. - so I thought -

Here is the Prophecy you can freely find online:

http://www.inthebeginning.com/articles/1965prophecy. htm

I PRAY YOU TAKE OUT TIME TO READ IT.

CHAPTER 16

Hysterectomy dream

I had a dream one night that I was being chased by a white cop car with its sirens going on top of the roof. I was running really fast in my dream to get away from the police who were in hot pursuit after me; running through bushes, between houses, over fences. I finally climbed really fast up the side of a tiny, little, white home and found myself lying on the floor covered up by a big piece of 'carpenter's' plastic with someone lying beside me although the Holy Spirit did not point out their identity. All of a sudden as a few people began to walk through this house, I sat up, pulled the plastic down to my waist, and said, 'I just had a hysterectomy'.

I had no idea what this dream meant and I actually had just had a hysterectomy surgery in real life. Things that happen to us in our lives will symbolically forewarn us of our future if we will allow the Holy Spirit to show us. Symbolically I had to have a physical hysterectomy because YHVH wanted me to go through a spiritual hysterectomy.

I was thinking this dream was a good dream showing me to keep on running from the Law of YHVH and not put myself under 'legalism' because this is what was indoctrinated into my mind from behind the pulpits since as far back as I can remember. I was taught 'We never want to put ourselves under legalism'. As it turns out, it was not a good thing that I was running from 'THE LAW'. Yeshua was warning me that I was running from YHVH'S Laws, all the while, living under Hasatan's rules and regulations. I was laying under the carpenter's plastic because Yeshua was a carpenter and Yeshua had to take me under some serious construction and 'cut out my history' so I could repent, Teshuvah, close doors to Hasatan, and get delivered. (hence hysterectomy: 'ectomy' meaning to cut out).

Please, hear what I am saying. You may be reading this book thinking this does not pertain to you. But unless you are keeping YHVH's Laws, keeping His Moedim, Keeping His Sabbath's and keeping them on the 7th day like HE Commands us, keeping His dietary Laws, keeping YHVH's Calendar and weaning off of the Gregorian time, Knowing how to bring in the new months by looking for the sliver of the moons, etc.. Then you are not keeping YHVH's Ways. You are still living under the rule and dominion of Hasatan and can't see it yet. Your blinders must come off for you to see it. They are called 'blinders' because they are able to completely blind you to the truth. Paul could not see clearly until his scales were removed from his eyes. Acts 9:18 NKJV Immediately there fell from his eyes *something like scales*, **and he received his sight at once;** and he arose and was baptized. Notice Paul could not see until his scales were removed from his eyes. That is how it is in the spiritual also. Satan has put his EVIL VEIL over our eyes and we are 'blinded' to YHVH's Truths. Repent and ask Abba Father to remove these blinders, veils, and scales in Yeshua's Name so you can begin to see clearly what the Spirit is saying to you. As it turns out, I had eyes but could not see because they were covered with scales. I had ears but I could not hear because they were stopped up with the lies from the pit of hell. My heart was stoney and uncircumcised and I could not understand the Ways of Almighty YHVH. I would have never guessed this about myself as I thought I was completely following The True Messiah. I never missed a church service, I was very active in our church, devoting all my time to the praise and worship ministry and then youth ministry. I was a 'good' person....in my own eyes....but not according to YHVH's EYES. It did not matter how 'holy' I 'thought' that I was. Let's not forget the fact that The Heavenly Father sent Yeshua on a mission in order to show me that my life was reflecting that of the harlot Gomer and to tell me that 'satan can't cast out satan'.. Why would HE tell someone so 'on fire' for YHVH and Yeshua something like this. Where was I going wrong.. Where I was going wrong, was I did not think the WORD was talking to me when it said we are stiff-necked and don't have eyes and ears to see and hear and that we've all gone a stray. I always thought it was talking about someone else, but never me. I went wrong by keeping all the 'traditions' of men that I was born into and never questioned what those holly days meant and how the wreath, xmas tree, ham, garland, the yule log, or the mistletoe represented our Messiah. I never questioned anything. There came a time that Yeshau began asking me every holly day, why I did what I did, cooked what I cooked, decorated how I decorated and what it all meant. I had no idea the answers to any of HIS questions so instead of answering HIM I just kept them in my heart and pondered them year after year.

Matthew 13:15
For the heart of this people has become dull,
With their ears they scarcely hear,
And they have closed their eyes,
Otherwise they would see with their eyes,
Hear with their ears,
And understand with their heart and return,
And I would heal them..

Abba Father's Desire is to send Yeshua to you also and show you where you are missing the mark just like HE did me. His Desire is to open your eyes and ears and heal you in every way. Do not harden your hearts to YHVH's Word, but rather allow His WORD to come and show you THE ONLY WAY, The ONLY TRUTH, and the ONLY way of LIFE and life more abundant.

Do not just continue to 'do' what you have been born into if you can not find it in THE WORD. Do not continue doing what some pastor behind a pulpit is telling you if you can not see it in YHVH's Word. If that pastor is telling you to not put yourself 'under legalism' or not to put yourself in 'bondage' by keeping YHVH's Laws - run away fast from that pastor and don't look back. Hasatan puts us in bondage. NOT YHVH'S LAWS. Ponder what you are even saying. This makes no sense to think that YHVH'S PERFECT LAW OF LIBERTY (James 1:25) could somehow put you in bondage. That is a most twisted lie from the pit of hell. YHVH brings us **out of the house of bondage** Exodus 20:2.

Psalm 40:6 ...My ears You have opened... YHVH can and will open your ears if you sincerely ask HIM to.. Each one of us must allow Yeshua to open our ears to hear what The Spirit is saying to us. We must stop being stiff necked and start questioning everything we do and question the meanings behind everything we've inherited from our forefathers: like our beliefs and traditions that we just keep passing down and have no idea why we do what we do. Do not think the bible is not speaking of you when you read that you are stiff-necked and your ears are always resisting the Holy Spirit and you continue to do the same 'traditions' that your forefathers have done and taught you. IT IS SPEAKING TO YOU. I did not think the bible was speaking about me either, but I was 'dead' wrong. I was living in the kingdom of darkness and it was leading me into death, hell, and destruction and I had no idea - while the curses were piling up on top of me.

Acts 7:51 You men who are stiff-necked and uncircumcised in heart and ears are always resisting the Holy Spirit; you are doing just as your fathers did.

There is hope if you are willing to repent and Teshuvah and go back YHVH's Ways and start obeying HIS Voice ONLY -then and only then will HE be your Elohim. You must first stop making Hasatan your ruler by doing what he wants you to do while you set Abba's Commands aside.

Jeremiah 7:23
But this is what I commanded them, saying, 'Obey My voice, and I will be your God, and you will be My people; and you will walk in all the way which I command you, <u>that it may be well with you.</u>'

Revelation 3:22
He who has an ear, let him hear what the Spirit says to the churches.

As you can imagine, anything being 'cut out' of a person is a very painful process to say the least. It is very difficult to crucify the flesh and walk after the SPIRIT of the Heavenly Father. The flesh and spirit war against each other constantly and neither one wants to give in to the other. A constant war is raging between good and evil, between the kingdom of LIGHT and the kingdom of darkness. We must constantly 17... be on our guard so that we will not be carried away by the **error of the lawless** and fall from our secure standing. 18 But **grow in** the grace/**favor** and **knowledge** of our Lord and Savior Yeshua Messiah. To Him be the glory both now and to the day of eternity. 2 Peter 3.

Notice that I emphasized the word favor versus grace. I believe we all need to understand this word a little better. It can change the way we think when we understand what YHVH really desires from us. YHVH does not just show 'favor' to anybody and everybody. We may find ourselves under His Divine Mercy and Compassion as not to completely give us what we deserve, but He does not look on us with 'favor' when we are a wayward child who has no desire to keep His Laws and keep covenant with Him. look at James 4:6 NASB ... '**GOD IS OPPOSED TO THE PROUD, BUT GIVES GRACE/ FAVOR TO THE HUMBLE.**' So for instance, if you are proud, you will not find favor with YHVH but will find yourself in opposition with The Father.

Isaiah 66:2 NIV These are the ones I look on with **favor**: those who are humble and contrite in spirit, and **who tremble at my word.** If we Truly trembled at HIS WORD, we'd be seeking His Word to see what it says and know we were living in error and we would tremble all the way back to YHVH's Ways. Here's something to tremble at; 2 Timothy 2:19 ONM Nevertheless the firm foundation of YHVH has stood, having this seal: **'YHVH must now know those who are His,** and everyone who names the Name of YHVH **must depart at once from unrighteousness.** How do we depart from unrighteousness unless we can discern between righteous and unrighteous, clean and unclean, holy and profane. We are actually commanded to know this. Are we any different than these priests and prophets of Zephaniah 3:4 NASB Her prophets are insolent, treacherous men; Her priests have profaned the sanctuary. **They have done violence to the Law.** How much violence are we doing to YHVH's Laws when most of us don't even care to know His Laws because we believe they've been done away with. We are supposed to be a kingdom of priests right now and if YHVH's 'most elect' in times past can be deceived, as the bible clearly says they were, what makes us think we have not been deceived along the way too. The Word says we've inherited nothing but lies and we know that Satan is a 'liar' and a 'deceiver' so why would we think he has not deceived us into following him by falling for a bunch of his lies. He deceived Eve and she was created far more spiritual than you and I are in our current fallen condition. He convinced Eve, somehow, that she should go against THE WORD YHVH had Instructed her and take the advice of a serpent instead.

Hasatan has convinced us that we need to keep Easter instead of PASSOVER. Hasatan has deceived us into thinking it is ok to change the 7th day Sabbath to the 1st day of the week (Sunday). To worship YHVH on 'the venerable day of the sun' when YHVH is clear that we are to set aside the 7th day as a sign between HIM and us. Satan deceived us into thinking we could eat whatever we wanted because YHVH's dietary Laws had been done away with - even though we are told to not add to or 'take away from' The Word.

Hasatan has us thinking that we can live however we want, doing what is right in our own eyes, because Yeshua is our Righteousness. YES, YESHUA IS OUR RIGHTEOUSNESS. This simply means that He is the ONLY ONE we must look at as our example of who to act like, talk like, look like, walk like, and He is the ONLY ONE Who showed us perfectly how to keep YHVH'S LAWS in order to walk a more abundant and blessed life. We are instructed to follow Yeshua - so why aren't we.

Ever wonder why you are not experiencing that more abundant life that Yeshua died to bring us.. Ever wonder why we find we are walking under a curse when **Yeshua became a curse for us Galatians 3:13.** Yeshau came to demonstrate how it is to be done so **if we are not walking using Yeshua as our perfect example**, then we are obviously not walking in YHVH's Ways. Therefore we put ourselves back under the **'curses on disobedience'** to YHVH's Word. Are you following Yeshua's demonstration of life and living by keeping the 7th day Sabbath just like our Messiah did, and by keeping all YHVH's Moedim (Feast Days) just like our Messiah did. Not keeping any traditions but only living by EVERY WORD that proceeds out of the Mouth of YHVH.

Yeshua asked me one time if I really thought the Father sent His Son to die a cruel death on the old rugged Cross just so we could all do whatever we wanted to do and not seek after the Righteousness of YHVH at all. It has turned into a free for all for YHVH's children. Every man doing what is right in their

own eyes and they don't even want to hear any bible scriptures that would make them feel convicted and even hint that
they would have to remove something from their lives in order
to repent, turn, and Teshuvah. Not many want to hear what I
have to say when I tell them we were never commanded to
keep these unscriptural holly days but that we are commanded
to keep HIS FEAST DAYS. (That not many keep because
they say 'they are not Jews.') Not many people want to come
out of their man-made traditions with all their nostalgic memories. Yeshua Himself tells us in John 8:12... Whoever **follows me** will not
walk in darkness, but will have the light of life. These man-made holly days
represent the kingdom of darkness and we are not following
Yeshua when we keep them because HE never kept them.
He kept Passover, not the pagan holly day Easter - named
after the goddess Ishtar, Eostre Ashtoreth, Inanna, Astarte,
Isis, 'the queen of heaven'. **Matthew 15:9** says **in vain do we worship
HIM, teaching as doctrines the precepts of men.** YHVH never instructed
us to keep something called Easter or christmas and we do
not see Yeshua keeping it, so how do we justify keeping these
pagan holly days that are devoted to other gods and goddesses. What part of **1 Kings 8:61** do we not understand: **Let your
heart therefore be wholly devoted to YHVH** our Elohim, **to walk in His statutes**
and to **keep His commandments,** as at this day.

You will find 'Easter' translated in one place in the Word and it
was translated incorrectly in Acts 12:4 in the KJV then it was
translated back to 'Passover' in the NKJV. The correct word
is Greek 3957 in the Strong's concordance: **Pascha** meaning
'the Passover'.

1 John 2:6 Whoever claims to abide in Him **must** walk as Jesus walked.

John 13:15 NASB For I (Yeshua) gave you an example, so that you also would do just as I (Yeshua) did for you.

Remember not everyone who says to HIM LORD, LORD will enter the kingdom of Heaven but will have to depart from Him because they were workers of lawlessness and the bible defines sin as lawlessness. Everyone who practices sin also practices lawlessness; and **sin is lawlessness** 1 John 3:4 NASB. So if you are not looking to see what YHVH says is righteous and Keep His Ways only, then you are 'lawless' and living in perpetual sin.

Obviously most of us do not live In Israel or near Jerusalem where YHVH placed His Holy Name. There is currently no temple making any part of sacrifices possible even if you were supposed to keep them. And who knows a Levite anyways because they were all carried into exile for forsaking and profaning YHVH's Laws. So I think we can safely say I am not talking about sacrificing animals. Hebrews 10 is very clear that Yeshua became our blood 'sacrifice' once and for all now for **it is impossible for the blood of bulls and goats to take away sins. Hebrew 10:4** NASB. But you should still read the entire Word and see what Abba's perspective is on things. He tells us what is proper and improper in His Eyes even through the Levitical priesthood. For example: **Numbers 5:11-31** talks about the 'adultery test' when the spirit of jealousy comes over a husband who suspects his wife has been unfaithful. So we can pick out verses that warn us of how dangerous adultery can be even though we do not take our problems to a Levite now. We now Have direct access to the Father through our Yeshua Messiah. We don't have to drink a literal drink of bitterness to see if the curse comes upon her. The Holy Spirit will see to it we drink a spiritual drink of bitterness because we are promised curses for being disobedient. We can clearly see through this passage, that if she is guilty she will bring a curse upon herself and there comes a time that she will be tormented from what she has done. The Law is very clear about 'blessings on obedience' and 'curses on disobedience'.

I had a dream once that I was walking around looking 9 months pregnant because my stomach had swelled (Numbers 5:21) and I saw a vision of myself letting my hair down (Numbers 5:18). Knowing what the bible says, The Holy Spirit was able to show me this was a warning about me actually cheating on my Husband Yeshua by straying from THE WORD... We can see the Father's mind as we notice the Word repeats over and over the woman who commits adultery **'defiles herself'**. I was walking around in total defilement by cheating on my Heavenly Husband, Yeshua, and not staying **'faithful'** to Him ONLY - by going a whoring and 'following' after Hasatan unawares. So we can get a good idea that Abba Father despises unfaithfulness to our spouses as well as unfaithfulness to our espoused Husband, Yeshua. Instead of taking everything to the Levite, we take everything straight to the Heavenly Father in prayer since through Yeshua the veil was torn in 2 to the Holy of Holies and Yeshua became the new High Priest in the order of Melchizedek -'My King Is **RIGHTEOUSNESS**'. Since Yeshua is now a High Priest of Righteousness, then HIS followers must come to **know** HIM- Know The Word- in order to **know** what is righteous and what is not. Then we can be that kingdom of priests...after Righteousness... that we are called to be. Remember also that vengeance belongs to YHVH and him alone because we will each be punished according to our sins. Even if we think we are 'just paying someone back for what they deserve'. **Proverbs 24:29 NASB Do not say, I shall do the same to**

him as he has done to me; I will repay the person according to his work. You are only giving way to the vicious cycle of sin that Hasatan is starting in your life if you allow him to make you think you have a right to take your own vengeance. Just take it to The Father and allow Him to handle it all. The Holy Spirit will handle it according to YHVH's Word every time on both sides of the marriage. There is nobody getting away with anything by the way. It seems like they are, when it takes so long to see their punishment or curse come to fruition, but make no mistake their day of reckoning is coming if they refuse to repent.

I had a vision that I was laying on the floor in front of my closet in the kitchen and Yeshua was performing open heart surgery. Even in my vision, I was able to feel the pain of the proce-dure. Spiritual open heart surgery can be very painful but it is an absolute necessity when our hearts are not right before YHVH. We each must allow YHVH to search our hearts and minds daily to show us what is in us. The Word says in Jeremiah 17:9 The **heart** *is* deceitful above all *things,* And **desperately wicked**; Who can know it. The Word doesn't lie so that means all of us need to ask the Father to replace our heart of stone with a heart of flesh that will beat with the Father's Heart.

Ezekiel 36:**25** I will also sprinkle clean water on you, and you will be clean. I will cleanse you from all your impurities and all your idols. **26** I will give you a new heart and put a new spirit within you; **I will remove your heart of stone and give you a heart of flesh. 27** And I will put My Spirit within you **and cause you to walk in** My statutes and to **carefully observe** My ordinances.

CHAPTER 17

One in 2 million

Don't let anyone tell you that Yehovah is not a Miracle Working YHVH. I remember the day Abba told me and my parents we were to sell both of our homes. I was renting from my parents, so my dad needed to sell both homes that were actually situated next door to each other. The **'chances'** my parents would sell these homes very speedily were very slim as they were at the higher end of the price spectrum. While praying about what Abba would have us do, my parents remembered a guy who had really liked one of their homes in the past. My dad reached out to them in an email to tell them he was getting ready to sell both homes if he was, by chance, interested. They took a while to respond back because they were on a cruise around South Africa, if I remember correctly. In the meantime, I had a dream or vision that I saw someone looking through a home. I saw black and white checkered flooring that was, in real life, in one of the homes, and I saw the sun room that was, in real life, in our other home, making a combination of both homes in one vision. All I heard were the words, **'2 million- I'll take it'.** Well, they were not quite that expensive, but my mom got **'1 in 2 million chances'** out of it. Sure enough, in the process of time, the man got back to my dad and said he'd be interested in looking through the homes before my dad listed the them through a realtor. The man said he'd take both homes and he cut my dad a check for both of them. He wanted his daughter and grandchildren to move in next door to him and his wife. What a Mighty YHVH we serve. With man, 1 in a 2 million 'chance' is near impossible, but with YHVH, **ALL THINGS ARE POSSIBLE.**

CHAPTER 18

We were going into limbo for a time

I could not believe it when my dad and my husband said we were going to move to the Hill Apartments. I remembered living there when I was about 7 years old, when we first moved to Springfield, Ohio. I did not have fond memories of this place. This is the place where a tree log fell on my head and knocked me out. Another memory I had was some scary old lady always trying to coax me into her apartment.

The Holy Spirit brought back to my remembrance a recurring dream I had about walking around the Hill apartments, over and over, and over. This, in fact, really did come to fruition after moving in. I would go out walking around the complex and pray everyday. This is how I found a lost cat named Long John and reunited him back to his owner. Abba finally convinced me this was His Perfect Will for us to move here. He told me we would be in 'limbo' for a bit of time. My parents were in Florida at the time, so I went to the office to check on openings. We had prayed that Abba would allow us to live close together as we lived side by side in the homes Abba just sold miraculously, and effortlessly. I stood there while the office manager checked on availability and was amazed at The Mighty Works of the Father, when she told me she had 2 units coming available right when we would need them. If that wasn't amazing enough, she proceeded to tell me they would both be on the same street called 'Limba' Dr. Yehovah is very symbolic. He told me we would be in 'limbo' for a time and He moved us right into 'limbo' and onto 'Limba'. He answered our prayers that we could live close together. We were almost right across the street from each other, not even 100 feet away. We would actually be closer now than the properties we were moving out of.

I know why I had trepidations about moving back into the Hill Apartments. The complex was rightfully named, as it sat right on top of a steep hill overlooking the city. After all, we are to be **a people set on a hill, whose light cannot be hidden** according to **Matthew 5:14**. Yeshua still had a lot of work to do in me and was sent by Abba Father to show me I was the **'imposter bride'** and not the **True bride** without spot or wrinkle. Yeshua showed me a vision of myself as a tiny little light lit up in the dark. I was so dim that I could barely see any light (even with complete darkness surrounding me). What light I had in me was flickering and about to go out. Yeshua was about to remove His Lampstand according to Revelation 2:5 - NKJV Remember therefore from where you have fallen; repent and do the first works, or else I will come to you quickly and remove your lampstand from its place—unless you repent.

The Holy Spirit was preparing me for the days ahead that would be most difficult that would cause me to cry out to Him continually.

I knew it was not going to be good, when my daughter and I went to borrow a key to the apartment so we could get some measurements to see what all we could bring. The Holy Spirit took me in slow motion as I was pulling into the complex that was situated on 'Faux Satin' Dr. How could this possibly turn out to be good, when we were about to live in a place where the main road was dedicated to the 'fake (faux), imposter, Satan/Satin', and how did I never see that before. When I see faux - I also hear, 'that ole fox'. Because someone who was not familiar with the pronunciation of the 'faux' could think it was pronounced 'fox'. I was contemplating what this was all about as we proceeded to head into the front room to measure when we saw a SNAKE in the 'family' room. Symbolic that I would soon be looking face to face at that 'ole serpent of old' called the devil. I called the office and she sent the maintenance man to catch the snake, who proceeded to behead it on our, soon to be, back porch. Now, you all may think this was all a coincidence, but I had learned enough to this point, to know when the Holy Spirit was pointing out and warning me what was to come. Hindsight is 20/20. Looking back, and knowing what I was about to go through, all of this was right on. I fought for my very life at this place when anxiety hit me so bad that I could not even function. It was here that I learned Hasatan had legal rights to me for so many reasons. It was here that I learned that a child of Yehovah can have a demon inside of them. And it was here that Yeshua taught me that 'Satan can't cast out Satan'. And that old lady trying to coax me into her apartment when I was a child was Satan in disguise trying to lure me in. I had a lot of repenting to do. A lot of learning to do. A lot of catching up to do. My entire life needed to make a 180 degree turn back to the Father in Yeshua's Name. This is called Teshuvah. The sad part is - I thought I was living for Yehovah and Yeshua already. Everything I did, I thought I was doing for the Glory of The Father and Yeshua. Come to find out, I was bringing dishonor to their Holy, Set Apart Names. But I did not drink, smoke, or cuss. I was a very friendly person. What was I doing that Yeshua would tell me the Words, 'Satan can't cast out Satan'. Why would HE tell me that. I will get to this, but first Abba had to take me out of my 'nursing profession', so I could **hold fast the 'profession of *my* faithfulness' without wavering (Hebrews 10:23** KJV). I had so much to learn and I had The Best Teacher in the whole world - My Yeshua Messiah, through the power of the Holy Spirit and HE would soon teach me how to decapitate the giants in my life just like my maintenance man decapitated that snake.

CHAPTER 19

Abba takes me out of my nursing career And supplies my very first paycheck

We are now moved into the Hill Apartments and Yeshua had much work ahead, so it was time to remove some obstacles that were hindering me from studying Abba's Word like I needed to. I was sitting outside on my bench swing looking around and I had a vision. During my vision, I heard Yeshua tell me I was to quit my nursing career. I figured I would pray about this for a little bit to make sure I was hearing correctly since this was kind of a big move. But Yeshua told me I needed to do it before my husband came home from work.

I proceeded to call my client's mother to put in my 30 day notice. She, of course, did not take it well and did not think I was hearing correctly. I was praying for some sort of confirmation that I, in fact, was doing the Will of my Father. Towards the end of the conversation, the client's mother had recalled something Abba had asked her the day before. She said she was walking through the house and she heard, 'What are you going to do without Michele'. That is all the confirmation I needed. I was already almost 100 percent certain I was doing Abba's Will. But this sealed it.

Of course, when my husband got home from work, he was in shock and awe and pretty upset to say the least. I told him it would be ok and that Abba would take care of us. My husband looked at me and said, 'Well God better supply your paychecks'. End of conversation.

About 1 week later, I was over in my parent's apartment having our home church service. Abba had taken us out of the church system by now, and we were doing church on our own just like the disciples in the Bible were also forced to do church out of homes. Everything goes full circle as YHVH works in circular 'cycles'. At first Abba allowed us to watch church services on tv but this soon stopped and we were led to do our own bible studies. While we were sitting there, my parent's landline phone rang. Since nobody answered the phone, the answering machine came on and I happened to hear and take notice that it was an Amber Alert for a cat named Long John. They proceeded to explain that Long John was a long haired, black and white cat.

After thinking to myself that I had no idea they did Amber alerts for pets, I did not think another thing about that message. After our home church, we decided to go take a walk around the apartment complex and pray as was our custom. As we were walking I happened to notice a cat that I had never seen before. I walked around this complex several times a day to pray and was very familiar with all the stray and feral cats running around. I immediately thought about the message I had heard about a black and white cat named Long John. I never thought it could possibly be Long John, but I felt compelled to look it up on my phone. Sure enough, Long John had a very distinct marking on his face. This, indeed, was Long John. I called the number and the man on the phone said to not lose this cat because it had a 500 dollar reward for it. He proceeded to say it belonged to his daughter who lived about 2 hours away in Indiana. The dad had accidentally let it out the door when his daughter had been there visiting. My mom was with me, and I told her to not let the cat go but the cat was not coming to us and was trying to hide in the bush beside the building. I immediately called the owner of Long John and she was so thrilled to hear that Long John was alive and was at my apartment complex. Without hesitation, she loaded up in her car and headed to our apartments, being familiar with the area having grown up around there. In the meantime, She had mentioned that Long John liked mayonnaise so I ran back to my apartment and got some mayonnaise to coax the cat out so we could grab it. To our dismay, the cat had escaped and we could not find it anywhere. The cat's owner was driving all the way from Indiana to Ohio to come get her cat that I could not find now. It was getting dark very quickly. By the time I knew it, the cat's owner was now with my mom and me as we were looking frantically for her cat. Walking around the apartment buildings at 11pm at night calling out for Long John. I finally asked the girl and my mom if we could just stop and pray. I began to pray and remind Abba that He had brought the animals to Noah to load them onto the ark. I asked Abba to bring Long John to us. It was way too dark to see a cat, and we did not even know where to look at this point with nothing but woods all around us. I will never forget, I turned around and saw a cat running towards us. I asked the girl if that was her cat and she said it was. Long John ran right to his owner and she picked him up. Now I was wondering how that cat would not just jump right out of her arms as we had a ways to go to get back to her car. I had remembered what her father said about having a reward. I did not feel ok about taking someone's money just for finding their cat. I was praying that only Abba's will be done and I kept hearing that I could accept the reward money because 'it was not her money'. When we got to the car, she told me that she rushed out of her home so quickly that she forgot the reward check. I told her that I did not want to take 'her money'. She insisted and said it was 'not her money' anyways that all of her friends and family chipped in to come up with the reward money. It was all in YHVH's Hands now. If He wanted me to have this money, then He would see to it that she mailed out the money to me. To my surprise, I received the check in the mail for 500 dollars. My very first paycheck since I quit my nursing career. Abba is so faithful. What a Mighty YHVH we serve.

Oh, and by the way. Abba has laid it on the hearts of some faithful servants to now give me their monthly tithes since they had quit going to a church and Abba has Faithfully supplied me with a monthly check ever since. It has now been 7 years and My Heavenly Father has not missed a single month of providing my paycheck.

CHAPTER 20

Abba doesn't care about money - He cares about our obedience to HIM

Let me show you how Abba will get His Way one way or the other. And He does not care how much money we lose to learn the lesson. On top of selling both homes, Yeshua instructed us from The Father that we were to get rid of most of our belongings and start over. So through prayer, dreams, and visions, we were led to go sell our items at a 'flea' market. Abba had to work a few 'bugs' out of us before we would be vessels used unto honor. **2 Timothy 2:21 NKJV Therefore if anyone cleanses himself from the latter, he will be a vessel for honor, sanctified and useful for the Master, prepared for every good work.** As it turned out, we were vessels to dishonor and did not even realize it. Isn't that all part of deception. You are deceived and do not know it because you are deceived. Hasatan puts a spiritual blindness over our eyes that we are unable to see the Truth. Hasatan doesn't want us to know the Truth, because **the Truth WILL set us free** from Hasatan's grips (John 8:32).

The deceiver puts an **evil veil** over our eyes. Hastan had taken me captive and I was doing his will when I didn't even know I was his prisoner. Abba had to send His Word to show me and my parents we were in error and needed to come to our senses and escape the evil veil that ensnared us.

2 Timothy 2:26 and *that* they may come to their senses *and escape* the snare of the devil, having been taken captive by him to *do* his will.

And oh how my POTTER had to shatter, squeeze, and smash this vessel and start all over creating a vessel unto Himself.

As the end of the day approached at the flea market, we had to make a decision as to if we would return the next day to sell any more items. We had a lot left and not one of us felt like returning the next day, or paying to rent our square for another day. Abba, once again, worked on our behalf as the lady right across from us made a living out of selling at the flea market so she offered to buy our items off our hands for 50 dollars. Meaning we would split the 50 dollars in half with my parents and just walk away, free from having to come back in the morning. Our husbands decided this was the way we would go when I happened to notice about 3 items that I knew were very expensive and did not plan to just leave these items with this lady for the amount of money she paid us. After all, I was not the one who made the agreement with this lady. I took an expensive trash can that you step on to open the lid, an otoscope I used in my nursing career, which was about 500 dollars alone, and my daughter's prom dress she was trying to sell which was about 600 dollars. Anyone who has had high school age daughters at a secular school knows how expensive prom dresses are. I paid a lot of money for this prom dress that she wore for a couple of hours. Abba did not care about how much any of these items cost me. A deal was a deal and YHVH's children must always walk in honesty and integrity. But my husband made the deal before I could throw these items into our truck. When I got home, I put the trash can upstairs in the bathroom. Very soon afterwards, I stepped on the pedal and it broke, never to work again. I immediately remembered I had **'stolen'** this item after the deal had been made with the lady. I finally had to throw that trash can away because I was reminded every single day of my 'greedy' little sin. I can't recall what ever happened to my daughter's dress but I do recall someone had an earache and when I went to get the otoscope out to look in their ears, it would not work. I plugged it in to charge it, and found it was dead as a door-nail and was no longer able to charge. Abba does not mess around. He will have a church without spot or wrinkle when He sends Yeshua back and He will no longer wink at our igno-rance nor tolerate sin in His own household (Acts 17:30). We are to trust in HIM ALONE and walk in honesty and integrity at all times. No matter what the circumstances. Doing what is right in HIS Eyes always. **Proverbs 10:2 warns us that 'ill-gotten gains do not benefit'** . It did not benefit me at all for taking those items home with me. They ended up in the trash and nobody got any use out of them at that point because of my 'greedy' little sin of ill gotten gain.

Everyone was out that money now, and I, alone, was left wal-lowing in my horrible guilt of my own sin.

Like I said, Abba had to show us in so many ways that money did not mean anything to Him. **1 Samuel 15:22 Obedience is better than**

sacrifice. We lost a lot of money by paying back debts of our former sins that we had never repented for.

Abba allowed us to think we were going to go out on the road and evangelize for Him right away. We went out, and my dad paid cash for a motorhome. Abba allowed my dad to put a lot of money into the RV to enhance its functionality such as solar, sway bars, etc.

I recall walking around the hills of my apartment complex one day and Abba showed me that He was going to have my dad roll that Rv over to me for free. My heart felt like it dropped to my feet at that moment. Standing there having a massive hot flash, I begged Abba not to make me relay this message and was pleading with Abba to show my dad Himself. Think about how awkward it would be to tell someone that 'Yehovah told me to tell you that you are supposed to give me an RV for free'. That sounds insane. I felt like the spoiled little girl named Violet on Willy Wonka and The Chocolate Factory- 'Daddy give me this RV NOW'. So I did not say one word about what Yeshua had relayed to me from the Father. But Yeshua kept relaying message after message letting me know I was accurate in Abba's Will for the RV to be given to me. I sat back and watched as my dad started experiencing a slew of very costly events in his business that he owned. The back tithes money from his business that he Owed Abba was the reason he was to give the RV to me. His employees were making huge, costly mistakes that were costing my dad copious amounts of money.

Since my dad would not pay tithes money on the profits of his business, then YHVH would see to it that the money would come out of the business one way or the other. If YHVH could not get any money from the profits then my dad would not make profits any longer. If he would not give me the RV as a form of back tithes money owed, then Abba would take it out in another form. Make no mistake.. Abba will eventually get His Way. We all need to start judging ourselves now before our Maker has to judge us because we refuse to do right. **1 Corinthians 11:31 NASB But if we judged ourselves rightly, we would not be judged.**

I remember one day at the gym, my mom had just told me of another costly error my dad's employees had made and was going to cost my dad about 26,000 dollars. As I was walking to my car, Abba asked me how long I was going to remain silent and not tell my dad what Yeshua had shown to me. Abba continued to tell me that He could charge my dad 3 times the price of that RV through these mishaps until he rolled the RV over to me. I could not stand to allow my dad to lose any more money. I immediately picked up my cell phone as I sat in the parking lot of the gym, and called my dad. I told him about all that Yeshua had shared with me and why Abba was causing all of these major expenses to arise until my dad was obedient and handed over the RV. To my surprise, my dad told me that Abba had been dealing with him on this very issue and that he had decided that morning that he was going to hand the RV over to me. Yehovah has the Final Say - Abba was finally getting the back tithes out of my dad that he had neglected to pay all his life. Abba doesn't care about money. He cares about our obedience and Yehovah will get His Way one way or the other. If we refuse to pay our tithes, Abba is not limited on how He decides to squeeze this money out of us. Tithes money does not have to be paid into the church system. Tithes can be whatever Abba tells us to do. He may tell us to give some-one money who is in need or buy someone something who does not have the money. Whatever you do, make sure you are led by the Holy Spirit.

Well, I did not get to keep this RV either. Number 1, anxiety struck me and I did not even want to step foot into that RV. When we finally moved off of Limba, we bought a house that reminded me of the movie, 'money pit'. Our home inspector missed some very important issues but the Father allowed it because **'this thing was from Yehovah' [1 Kings 12:15, 24].** I was never meant to keep the RV and Abba knew I would need to sell it to get the money to fix all the problems in our home.. and then we went out with the leftover money and squandered it on decorations for the home *just **before*** Abba began teaching me about occult symbols and the dangers of having them in our homes. As it turns out, every last piece of my decor had to be tossed out and destroyed. If it did not have any occult symbols, then Abba showed me it was a fake imposter, void of life, made to look like what Abba had created and given life to. -Like all of my fake plants.- And I had a lot of them. The world has gotten so good at making these fake imposters, it is very difficult to tell the real plant from the imposter plant. Hasatan is an imposter who poses as an Angel of light trying to pose as Yeshua. Can we tell the difference between the True Yeshua and the imposter Satan. You would think the answer would be, 'yes, it is obvious'. But it is not obvious. If we keep coming into agreement with the kingdom of darkness and having all his garbage in our homes, we will not be able to tell the difference, because this is one of the ways Hasatan gains legal right to us. We are agreeing that we would rather have the *'imitation'* in our homes that does not contain any form of life at all rather than have the 'real deal' created by Yehovah Himself. We seem to be completely content having death sitting all around our homes mirroring Hasatan's kingdom. Whatever happened to the bible verse NASB **'Your kingdom come. Your will be done, On earth as it is in heaven** Matthew 6:10. How can we bring the Kingdom of Heaven into our homes if it is crammed full of the kingdom of darkness. As a matter of fact, anytime we come into agreement with Hasatan and his deceiving kingdom, he gains legal right to us in that particular area. So if we want to 'deceive' the world by our fake, deceiving plants sitting all around us, representing the imposter, Satan - Then Hasatan will, in turn, be able to 'deceive' us so we can't *discern* between the True life giving Yeshua and the fake imposter that brings death. The Word says in Deuteronomy 30:15 <u>Amplified</u> **Listen closely, I have set before you today life and prosperity (good), and death and adversity (evil).....** Deuteronomy 30:19 <u>NAS</u> **I call heaven and earth to witness against you today, that I have placed before you life and death, the blessing and the curse. So <u>choose life in order that you may live</u>, you and your descendants.**

Yehovah is very clear on His Instruction to us to **'choose life so we may live'**...*and our decisions not only affect us but also our descendants*. Our children absolutely suffer because of our bad choices. ‒ Numbers 14:33 NASB Also, your sons will be shepherds in the wilderness for forty years, and **they will suffer *for* your unfaithfulness,** until your bodies perish in the wilderness. So why do we continually 'choose' to surround ourselves with death. It matters not of all the reasons, excuses, and justifications you may have for preferring the fake plant over the live plant. We are still supposed to obey Abba's Word over our own desires every time without exception.

Hasatan always has an agenda behind everything he does. He chooses the 'plant' to defile because we are supposed to follow the 'plant' of righteousness, our Yeshua Messiah. Yeshua is the vine and we are the branches. Isaiah 61:3 NASB ..**So they will be called oaks of righteousness, The planting of the LORD, that He may be glorified.** So do you want to be an offshoot of Hasatan or Yeshua... We can clearly see we are glorifying Hasatan by having these 'fake plants' that represent death and not life and righteousness. Take a look at **Enoch 93:2... 'Concerning the children of righteousness and concerning the elect of the world, And concerning the plant of uprightness, I will speak these things...**some translations you may find it in Enoch 92)..

So can you see why the devil would want to make fake plants for us to come into agreement with by bringing them into our homes.

I am not trying to turn your life upside down by throwing curve balls at you in every chapter but Yeshua has been sent on a mission through The Power of The Holy Spirit to show us these very deceptions that are bringing destruction upon our-selves and our loved ones. Hasatan never 'clearly' advertises his plans to kill , steal, and destroy us - but we know he is pur-posed in his heart to accomplish just that by taking advantage of the fact that we are ignorant to what is of YHVH and what is of the kingdom of darkness. 2 Corinthians 2:11 NABRE so that we might not be taken advantage of by Satan, for **we are not unaware of his purposes.**

Wouldn't it be wonderful if Hasatan was required to put his warning label on these products we are bringing into our homes, that said:

WARNING: 'You are about to buy an item devoted to destruction / devoted to Hasatan so he will gain legal rights to destroy you - so buy at our own peril. thanks in advance - hope to see you in hell'

BUT WE DON'T HAVE THAT CONVENIENCE. We now have The Holy Spirit attempting to lead and guide us into all TRUTH and to show us what is of YHVH and what is of the kingdom of darkness if we would actually pay attention. Most people push the prompting of the Holy Spirit out when they don't want to make a change or they don't want to know what The Holy Spirit is trying to show them because it makes them feel uncomfortable.

There is the **True Bride** of Messiah, without spot or wrinkle, and there is the **imposter bride** that goes a whoring after anything and everything their little heart desires without any concern what is pleasing or displeasing to The Heavenly Father - without caring to discern what is clean and unclean, Holy or profane. We think we are serving the True Messiah, but are, in fact, an offshoot of Hasatan, serving the imposter, the devil, in everything we do - becoming **'the plant of unrighteousness'**. And we profane YHVH's Holy, set apart Name in the process.

Ezekiel 39:7 NASB And I will make My Holy Name known in the midst of My people Israel; and **I will not allow My Holy Name to be profaned anymore.** But the nations will know that I am the LORD, the Holy One in Israel.

Yehovah is done allowing us to call ourselves HIS child then turn around and profane HIS Holy Name by doing the very things HE HATES. Yeshua has been sent on a mission to clean up His True Bride to make her spotless and blameless before The Father. The Father is not going to allow HIS PERFECT, SINLESS SON to marry a harlot.

We don't even see any harm in the things we are doing. The Word warns us in **Jeremiah 16:19 that we've inherited nothing but falsehood, futility, and things of no profit.** And we don't even know it because we are deceived. Being deceived is a real problem. You have no idea you are deceived, because you are deceived. What a mess. If not for the Mercy and compassion of our Father through our Messiah, searching all the Earth for hearts that are wanting to come His Way, there would not even remain a remnant of the True YHVH.

I had to destroy and throw out every last decoration we had bought with the RV money. Abba doesn't care about money. He cares about our obedience to Him and His Word. As a matter of fact, throwing all that money down the drain was all part of my test. YHVH could have taught me about symbols and occult objects *before* I bought all those decorations, but He clearly waited for me to purchase all the decor I had money for, toss the price tags in the garbage, put holes in my walls and get everything looking real nice, *and then* He decided to show me these truths. It made it all the harder to go His Way at this point. Especially dealing with my husband who was not on board with my new walk with Yehovah. Abba was very gracious though. He allowed me to pay off my daughter's car with my tithes money from the sale of the RV. Yeshua also instructed me to pay cash for my grandma's little Chevy Spark that she could no longer drive because she was losing her eyesight and was afraid to get behind the wheel any longer. I did not want to buy her car, but Abba finally let me know this was His Perfect Will so I finally came into alignment with The Father's Will. This little car was such a blessing to me and the fact that Sparks are very good on gas was just an added bonus. Praise YHVH. It wasn't what I thought I wanted but Abba knew what I needed. Especially when the price of gas jumped up to over 4.00 per gallon and knowing my little spark could be filled for around 25.00 instead of 100.00. Abba knows exactly what He is doing.

I could tell you so many stories just like these. But I think you get the picture. And I repeat ...'**to obey** *is* **better than sacrifice'**... 1 Samuel 15:22 KJV. Abba does not care about money. He wants us to be obedient to HIM and to HIS WORD. His Word plainly tells us we are **blessed on obedience and cursed on disobedience. Deuteronomy chapters 11 and 28** are good examples of this. Look at all the curses my dad endured before he was obedient in giving me the RV.

Oh and by the way, we can't make up our own ways of what is right and wrong. Abba has already laid this out in HIS WORD from Genesis to Revelation.

Proverbs 14:12 **There is a way** *which seems* **right to a person, But its end is the way of death.** It seemed perfectly fine to me to have these fake plants all through my home. It was not until the Holy Spirit wrote on my heart and told me it was displeasing to The Father and showed me that this was one method that Hasatan gains access to us.

We all must allow Romans 10:2-3 to sink in:**2... they are zealous for God, but not on the basis of knowledge. 3 Because they were ignorant of God's**

<u>righteousness</u> and <u>sought to establish their own,</u> they <u>did not submit to God's</u> <u>righteousness.</u> I had a zeal for YHVH, but I did not KNOW that how I was serving Him was not HIS WAYS and I was displeasing Him in the process. Yehovah's Ways are right. Not our ways. Not man made traditions. Not rules made up by men. Not doctrines of men. Matthew 15:8 **'These people honor Me with their lips, but their hearts are far from Me. 9 They worship Me in vain; <u>they teach</u> as doctrine <u>the precepts of men.'</u>** I was worshiping Him in vain. I was whoring after the devil and did not realize it. Everything I did was bringing glory to Hasatan and the kingdom of darkness. We must get back to worshiping The Father in the Ways He has instructed us to live for HIM. HE LEFT US WITH THE GREATEST INSTRUCTION MANUAL WE COULD EVER HAVE - THE BIBLE - HIS WORD - THE WORD MANIFESTED INTO REAL LIFE FLESH AND BLOOD TO BECOME OUR PERFECT EXAMPLE OF HOW TO LIVE THIS LIFE - OUR **'E MANUAL' (EMANUEL)** THAT IS NOW **DOWNLOADED** AND WRITTEN ON OUR HEARTS THROUGH THE PROMISED HOLY SPIRIT.

CHAPTER 21

Struck with severe Anxiety for 3 years

While still living at the Hill Apartments, a lot happened during our time in limbo. Let me tell you about one of the worst times in my entire life and it was only by the Grace of Yehovha that I even made it out alive. I saw in a vision, my toe being tagged in a morgue. This is what happened.

One day as I was walking the trash to the main dumpster, I saw a vision. I saw several demons inside a body flowing quickly through what was known to be the serotonin. I said out loud, 'Oh, that can not be good.' I had noticed the evil looks on the demon's faces. They were viscous and out to cause some real damage. I would soon come to realize that it was definitely not good, and learned that it was actually *me* the demons were inside. I felt as though my heart sank to my feet as I asked Abba if I was saved because I was taught that no child of YHVH could have a demon inside of them. He proceeded to tell me that He was dealing with my everyday walk, sanctification, and obedience to The Father.

I was standing in the bathroom brushing my teeth one night when I received a text from someone who heard we had gotten an RV. You know, the one my dad was instructed to *give* us -**FOR FREE**. The RV was parked at my dad's shop at his business because we obviously could not park it at the apartments -so nobody knew we had an RV. I was asked to text a pic of the RV. As soon as I sent the 'image', I knew that it was displeasing to Abba but I continued to brush my teeth, when they texted right back and asked me to send a different picture- this time of the inside'. Look, I have no idea what was wrong with me, but I sent a 2nd 'image' after knowing the 1st 'image' was a stench in YHVH's Nostrils. Once again, I felt a warning from the Holy Spirit. You would think I would have stopped brushing my teeth and began repenting immediately, but remember, I was coming out of the church system and Yeshua had a lot of brainwashing, wrong doctrine, and programming to get out of me so at the time I did not know I was supposed to officially repent. So instead, I continued brushing my teeth. Not a surprise when I received the 3rd text asking me to send a pic of the TV. I sent the pic... Immediately my heart smote me and I had the feeling of overwhelming disaster was going to strike me from my disobedience and pride. But I still did not go fall on my knees and beg and plead with Abba to forgive me of my 3 sins. There are 3 types of sin. **'Sin'** that we commit in error (the first pic), **'Iniquity'** that we commit deliberately (the second pic), then **'transgression'** which we commit to anger Yehovah (the third pic). As I was heading to my bedroom, my heart felt like it stopped beating and I just about lost consciousness. I leaned over onto the bed and my heart finally started beating again just seconds away from blacking out. I was having marital problems at the time, so of course my husband did not even ask what was wrong with me but just looked straight ahead at his tv. This was not the first episode like this. I have since learned that it is demonically induced and I can immediately bind them and cast them to the abyss as long as I am repented up. This happened to show me **my heart was not right** and was not a heart beating unto life towards my Heavenly Father in Yeshua's Name but, instead, it was a heart 'failing' unto death as I was doing what Hasatan wanted me to do, meanwhile setting aside the commandments of YHVH, which gave the devil legal right to mess with my heart.

Abba told me that since I was 'so anxious' to send not 1 pic, but 3 pics, that I would be struck with 3 years of severe anxiety. 1 year for every pic. I did not think too much about it, because I could not imagine how badly Abba Father would actually allow me to be struck. Remember I was not taught in church to repent about these kinds of things but that Yeshua covered it. I was taught that Yeshua 'finished it all' on the cross and that I did not need to do anything but keep my faith in Yeshua and what He did on the Cross for us. I had no idea it was about my **'faithfulness'** to my Heavenly Father through my Yeshua.

I actually was not struck that day, and had forgotten all about it.

One day as I was standing in my bedroom I saw a demon coming towards me. I did not know how to stop it or what to do and I remembered the Bible saying **resist the devil and he will flee James 4:7.** What did that even mean exactly. I had no idea how to resist something that I could not even see and that had supernatural powers which I did not seem to have at the moment. I had never been taught spiritual warfare- EVER. So I told it to flee in Yehsua's Name. It paused for a moment and then got closer. I told Abba it was not listening to me right as the demon entered into me and disappeared inside my chest. I asked Yeshua what just happened and why the demon ignored me. Yeshua told me in plain Words, 'Satan can't cast out Satan'. Once again, I said, 'So does that mean I'm not saved.' Yeshua continued, 'You have too much darkness in you and a house divided cannot stand.'

Notice I kept asking Yeshua if I was 'saved' - not understanding that our salvation was an ongoing, everyday process of 'being saved' according to our faithfulness to our Heavenly Father. It is not a one time altar call to 'give your heart to the Lord'. If you truly give your life over to The Master then you will be faithful to HIM all the days of your life.

Where did I go so wrong. **James 4:6 ...God opposes the proud, but gives grace to the humble. 7 Submit yourselves, then, to God. Resist the devil, and he will flee from you. 8 Draw near to God, and He will draw near to you. Cleanse your hands, you sinners, and purify your hearts, you double-minded.** Let's break these verses down. Right off the bat, It was strike number 1 when it clearly says **YHVH opposes the proud**. Yikes. You never want YHVH on your opposing team. But apparently I could not **'resist' the devil**'s temptation and ended up being on 'team satan'. I failed miserably in **submitting myself to my creator**. I struck out big time. I just **made the Word of Elohim of none effect. (Mark 7:13)** I was partaking in pride by sending those pictures as if it was some big 'status symbol' - an RV that I did not even buy to begin with - but now I would 'pay' for it.

Let's not gloss over verse 8 about **cleansing your hands 'you sinners'
and purify your hearts 'you double minded'**.

I could not refute the Word that I was clearly a sinner and
double minded by saying with my lips I serve YHVH, but in my
actions I was serving Hasatan. Actions do speak louder than
words. Isaiah did correctly prophecy about **ME**. I could start to
see how the Bible was talking about me now and not everybody else. I was not only a double minded sinner, but now I
could add hypocrite to the list. Yeshua Himself reminds us of
this but I always thought He was talking about everyone else
but me. **7 You hypocrites. Isaiah prophesied correctly about you: 8 'These
people honor Me with their lips, but their hearts are far from Me. Matthew 15:7.**

I could not even take this case to the Courts of Heaven. It
would be thrown out immediately. What part of **2 Samuel 22:21** did
I not understand. **YHVH has rewarded me according to my righteousness;
He has repaid me according to the cleanness of my hands.** Let's reverse
this statement.. So I got paid for my unrighteousness and
unclean hands. Not my finest moment for sure. **Job 17:9 Yet a
righteous one holds to his way, and the one with clean hands grows stronger.**
Through my non-compliance to YHVH's Word I was proving
that I was not holding to righteousness. As it turns out my
hands were filthy because I was not able to demonstrate one
ounce of 'strength' against that demon but was completely
helpless. Instead of growing stronger as a child of YHVH
is promised, I had become completely helpless, weak, and
emaciated and did not even know it. Here's another excerpt
from the WORD that I thought was written to everyone but
me. **Isaiah 1:4 Oh, sinful nation, people weighed down with guilt, Offspring
of evildoers, Sons who act corruptly. They have abandoned YHVH, They have
despised the Holy One of Israel, They have turned away from Him. 5 Where will**

you be stricken again, As you continue in your rebellion. The entire head is sick and the entire heart is faint. 6 From the sole of the foot even to the head There is nothing healthy in it, Only bruises, slashes, and raw wounds; Not pressed out nor bandaged, Nor softened with oil. I was so ill and did not even realize it. I had been born into deception. But I still knew Abba Father was displeased with sending those pics and I alone made all 3 choices to attach those pics and hit send. I had nobody to blame but myself. YHVH rewarded me according to my righteousness; according to the cleanness of my hands hath he recompensed me. (Psalm 18:20). But Job 22:30 says He will deliver even one who is not innocent, rescuing him through the cleanness of your hands. Here I am supposed to be rescuing others through the cleaness of my hands, and I can not even deliver myself -what was going on. I needed to realize I was obeying Hasatan's agenda in everything I did, meanwhile setting Abba's Instruction 'E-Manuel' aside. In the process I was appointing Satan to be ruler over me. Romans 6:16 is pretty clear. NASB Do you not know that the one to whom you present yourselves as slaves for obedience, you are slaves of that same one whom you obey, either of sin resulting in death, or of obedience resulting in righteousness.

What darkness was in me and what was causing my hands to be unclean. Well let's see. I just witnessed a very dark demon enter into me. Why did that happen and how many more of those things have snuck into me unawares. I was a really 'good' person who devoted their entire being to Yehovah and Yeshua - or so I thought. How was I a house divided. I thought that I had made my decision quite clear whom I had chosen to serve. My mind was not confused on who I wanted to serve. I wanted no part of the kingdom of darkness. But what I did not realize is that **my entire life was aligned with the kingdom of darkness**. Until I figured this out and learned how to walk in the Ways of Yehovah, I was not going to have **any** power, authority, or dominion over any power of darkness out alone **all** the powers of darkness. **Luke 10:19 NASB Behold, I have given you authority to walk on snakes and scorpions, and _authority_ over all the power of the enemy, and nothing will injure you.** I had to realize and admit that YHVH's Word was not seeming to apply to me when it came to promises of blessings and life. WHY NOT.. And the kingdom of darkness was injuring me badly -when The Word says it won't. HOW COULD THIS BE..

I had to be shown the TRUTH before I could make an informed decision on whom I was going to serve. If I chose YHVH, then to YHVH I should live unto life and blessings, but if I chose the kingdom of darkness, then I could expect a life leading to curses and death. And from the looks of it I was reaping exactly what I had sown all my life - death and curses.

I recall an instance right before YHVH had taken me out of my nursing career. One very early morning as I was getting out of my car to go into my client's home my phone started playing on its own out of nowhere. The song I heard was, 'the chimes of time ring out the news, Another day is through. Someone slipped and fell, was that someone you.' The song continued to play and I had no way to shut it off, because no app was opened on my phone and I had no idea where this song was coming from. But what I do know is the Holy Spirit pointed out 'someone slipped and fell, was that someone you'. Of course I did not think it was me. I did not live my life in total rebellion -at least the kind of rebellion that was obvious to me. The song played a little bit and then it just stopped on its own. I pondered what had just happened and why it happened. I knew the Holy Spirit was trying to show me something, but what that something was, I had no idea. I had forgotten all about the picture incident and could not imagine *'that some-one'* was me who had slipped and fallen. A lot of people came to mind of who the song was referring to but my name was not on that list. I thought my life was pleasing to YHVH.

We do ourselves no favors by refusing to believe that we are the sinner the Holy Spirit is talking about.

I will tell you another instance where even more demons came into me, to lay dormant, until the anxiety was to strike. I was laying in bed one night wide awake. I assumed my husband was asleep because he never moved or said one word of what I will share with you. My Uncle had recently passed and I was given the wind **chime** from his funeral which was hanging on our shed just below our bedroom window. Our window happened to be open that night. Out of nowhere, I heard the wind blowing as if I was hearing something straight from a horror show. I heard an eerie sound of what the world would call 'ghosts'. Then I heard them blow through the windchimes and make the chimes clang together. The next thing I know, my ceiling is polka dotted with demons. They covered my entire ceiling like black and white camouflage. They started one by one, coming down my wall towards my pillow and then disappeared. For some ridiculous reason, I thought they must have entered into my husband even though I clearly saw them come straight down onto my pillow and disappear. He was the obvious 'sinner' in our home not caring at all about the Ways of Yehovah. I never imagined they were entering me. I thought my entire life was wrapped up in my Savior and Father. How could they be entering a child of YHVH anyways when I had been taught all my life that they could never enter a child of the Most High. In fact, they did enter me. I have learned they will lay dormant as long as they need to so that the child of YHVH will not suspect that the demons are in them for fear the believer will start asking questions and learn to clean up their lives and cast these destroyers out of them. The last thing these demons want is for the host to repent, Teshuvah, and bind and cast them out before their job there is finished.

On a side note: so called 'ghosts' are spirits. But we must discern from which kingdom any spirit is from. Spirits of darkness love to manifest and gain entrance through things that blow air for the fact that a 'spirit' is 'wind, breath, or air'. This comes from Ruach a Hebrew word from strong's concordance 7307. So if you learn what occult symbols look like, you will start noticing that your home's air ducts are wrapped up in insulation with occult symbol patterns all over them giving demons legal right to flow through your home's air ducts. Ceiling fans blow 'air', so demons love to hang out on them and make sure they are equipped with lots of symbols. Car vents will sometimes have HEXagons behind the openings for demons to blow out into our face. Front bumper ventilation to automobiles will usually have some sort of diamond pattern or HEXagons for the air to enter along with all the demons that are being summoned into your vehicle by these demon summoning symbols. The list goes on.

My son had finally agreed to go camping with me as long as he could take some friends along. I was out running some last minute errands and was preparing to leave in just a little bit. As I was driving to the park to pray first, I heard Yeshua tell me the words, 'This is that'. Of course I said, 'This is what' but with no response. I had no idea what 'that' even meant. But I was about to learn. I was heading home to go pick up my son and his friends so we could head to my birth town of Van Wert, Ohio in the RV to go camping so I could help my Aunt.

I was heading down the highway and looked into the **rear**view mirror at **my son** and **his friends** and I immediately remembered a dream I had of being in the RV with my son and all hell breaking loose, even to the point of being stranded along the road. Suddenly it felt like the demons shut off my windpipes and lungs and an elephant was now sitting on my chest. I can't even explain the awful feeling of anxiousness that hit me out of nowhere. I had to keep turning the A/C up full blast and blowing it on my face to even get a breath. I did not know about occult symbols at the time so I imagine I was being pumped full of demons from the 'air' system as well. Here I am driving down the road in the RV, with all these boys under my care, along with my 2 cats that hated road trips, and I could not even function to take care of myself at this point. Oh... and by the way...**'THIS WAS THAT'** that Yeshua was warning me about earlier that day.

Allow me to share the symbolism:

— 'rear' 'view' mirror - 'viewing' or looking at a sin that was behind me in my past (rear).

— Remember the 'images' I sent - you 'view' pics. I sent the pics of the RV - so of course it would hit me while I was driving the RV. Hasatan has legal right to us according to our specific sins. This is how you can learn what your sin is if you are unaware of the sin beforehand. You can look at what you are specifically going through and seek the Holy Spirit to show you what specific sin or sins you need to repent for.

So if you kick your dog in anger, expect the punishment to have to do with feet. Like your own foot or like the dog 'paws' dragging in mud all over your carpet in the exact spot you kicked your dog. NO, I did not just pull that example out of thin air. No, I do not go around kicking my dogs either. I was having a very stressful day, and living with my mother-in-law with 6 animals that kept running through the sliding door into the rest of the house everytime I opened the door. She was not exactly a lover of pets. Especially my 4 very large, hyper dogs. My son kept telling me I needed to be more forceful with them because I was the only one that seemed to not be able to get through the door. Obviously Hasatan was in full out war mode with the '**spirit** of frustration' all over me. We should never allow ourselves to be angry and frustrated to the point of losing control. I should have binded the spirits of frustration and anger before I allowed them to trip me up. Notice that frustration is not just a 'feeling'…it is a literal 'spirit' that causes you to feel frustrated. **Genesis 4:7 warns us that 'sinful things' are waiting and lurking to trip us up, but we must master them**. Most translations translate it into 'sin', but 'sinful thing' is also a translation for the same Hebrew word. Strong's 2403 - Chattah`ah - 'sinful thing' or 'sin'.

I did not kick the dogs to hurt them, but my heart smote me for losing control to the point that I would kick towards them at all. I immediately let them outside and ran to my bedside, fell to the floor with tears running down my face and began repenting and begging Abba to forgive me. I have been warned by Abba not to hit my dogs. I once broke my hand for breaking that command while trying to break up a fight between my 2 male pit bulls. And It was a long healing process to be able to use my hand again. It has been over a year, and I still have weakness and pain in it from time to time even up into my wrist. I let the dogs back in and went back to the bed to pray some more. I noticed that my dog 'Webster' had mud on his feet. I looked at my bed and there was mud on my bed. I got up to look at the floor. Sure enough, there were paw prints on the floor. But the worst of the muddy paw prints were right where I had kicked the dogs back with my foot. I actually thanked Abba for my punishment. Without having repented, my punishment could have been very severe. Of course Hasatan used my dog **Web**ster because symbolically, he caught me in the **'web'** he spun for me. I got caught in the snare of hasatan instead of mastering the demons sent on assignment against me. Remember these demons are lurking all around trying to trip us up constantly so they can gain access in whatever way we give them. I did happen to stub my bare foot on the bathroom door that evening before washing and getting clean.

Back to the anxiety: I had no idea how I was to ever survive 3 years with this severe anxiety when I did not think I would even make it through the next hour. But that was not the worst of the trip. I managed to get through the stay at the campground and then the day came to head home. We were on our way. My GPS was on because I was unfamiliar with the area. I knew the RV would not fit under certain bridges. I also knew that because I was towing a car behind us, that I was not able to back the camper up without unhooking the car completely. So as I was driving down the road, I happened to notice a bridge ahead. Kind of looked like a small, 1 lane bridge, but was very hard to tell. At that moment my phone rang and took me off of GPS. My Aunt was calling me and I had to answer the phone so I could get back onto my GPS. I decided my RV would not fit through the bridge ahead, and since I could not back the RV up while towing the car, I hurried and turned into a church parking lot. This is when I heard the most horrific scraping sound against the RV that I never want to hear again. I got out and was looking to see what had just happened when I noticed the church had put a very thick metal wire up across the entrance and I could not see it from so far up in the RV. What a disaster. Not to mention I just broke a church's wire they had put across the entrance of their parking lot. I got out and went up to the church to tell someone what I had done to offer and pay for the damages but all the doors were locked and I was not able to breathe. The air was so muggy that I felt like I was breathing underwater without scuba equipment. My body struggled for each breath I managed to take.

— Symbolism of breaking the metal at a church and causing damage to my RV:

— I was 'Metaling' in the kingdom of darkness when it came to my walk with The Father through Messiah

— 'breaking' my hedge of protection

— and it was giving Hasatan legal right to cause 'damage' to me.

— the RV standing for 'rendezvous' - because I was having a 'rendezvous' with Hasatan while I was

'cheating' on my Yeshua who I am espoused to
marry.

I had my suspicions that Abba was trying to show me something in earlier years when I had purchased my rendezvous
car. The steering was going bad on it as well as the breaks.
Symbolism - I could not seem to STOP being so careless in
steering my life in the wrong direction.

I got back into the RV and drove away and had no idea where
I was going now. My Gps seemed not to be working either on
top of everything else. (symbolism - because I had no clue
what direction I was spiritually heading) I turned onto **Chapel**
Road and Immediately realized this had been a huge mistake.
I saw cars just sitting on the road while a very long train was
stopped in the middle of the tracks. I sat there for a while as I
watched car after car do a U turn and leave. Well this RV was
not doing a U turn in the middle of this narrow road. I saw a
gravel turn around at the end of the road just to the left of the
train tracks. So I drove down and was turning the RV around
and realized I was going to have to drive though about 5 feet
of some tall grass in order to make the complete turn without
backing up at all and having to unhook the car. I saw something yellow through the grass so I stopped the RV and got out
to realize there was an immovable, yellow fire hydrant **sitting
in my way** to finish making the turn. Just a sign from Hasatan
to let me know he got me yet again. First I scratch the RV up
by breaking through some thick metal to a **church** parking lot
of all places and now I am at a stand still on **Chapel** Rd with a
big yellow apparatus sticking out of the ground. Yeshua is our
living water to put out the fire of the enemy. What was Abba
trying to cause me to see. For starters, I needed to 'stand still'

and know which god I was serving and realize it was **me** the demons were after. There are no coincidences in life, and the Holy Spirit was going to get through to me one way or the other no matter how long it took and how much torturing I had to go through in the process. That is why I could not seem to get through no matter which way I took. Because symbolically the Holy Spirit 'could not get through' to me either. I kept thinking The Father was trying to show me somehow that my husband was the sinner. But all the while, He was trying to get my attention to help me see the wretched mess that I was. I could not even see it because of all the false doctrine, lies, deception, and brainwashing that I had undergone since I was old enough to comprehend.

By this time, I really thought I would pass out from lack of oxygen. And let's not forget, I still had my son and his friends under my care. Oh yeah. And my 2 cats that had not eaten the entire trip because they HATED road trips. It was inevitable at this point, I was forced to unhook the car I was towing. I gave my son my keys to the car and told him and his friends to drive it home. I could not be responsible with these boys in my care any longer with my severe anxiety and was not sure I would make it much longer.

There is a praise report out of all of this mishap. I had been in Rural King just days prior to my trip and Yeshua told me to buy a pair of rubber rain boots and put them in the camper and told me 'I would be glad I did'. I was so glad I decided to be obedient this time. Because I failed to mention when I got out of the Rv to unhook my car, I was standing in muddy water up to my shins. Abba is so Gracious even when we do not deserve it. I had headed out that morning without eating breakfast, and now my blood sugar seemed to be dropping quickly. By the time I got back into the RV from unhooking the car and sending my son and his friends on their way, I was absolutely drenched in sweat from the hot muggy weather. I was so nauseated from anxiety that I had no idea what I could keep down, but I knew I had to make myself eat something before I backed up and headed down the road to find a different route. The last time I checked, the train was still stopped on the tracks so I was trying to force something down to raise my blood sugar when I heard a knock on my door. I looked out and saw a cop car with its lights on. This is not what I wanted to deal with right now with my anxiety feeling like it was killing me with a slow, agonizing death and now this didn't help matters at all. I tried my best while struggling for every breath to explain what was going on. Apparently seconds before the cop arrived the train had pulled away with no trace of a road blockage at this point. He seemed to believe me anyways and he pulled away, not at all alarmed by my state of health. This was the longest, most difficult drive I have ever driven. I really thought I would not make it home. When I was about 40 minutes from where I stored the RV, I could not make it another mile. I pulled over into what seemed to be an abandoned business. The parking lot was empty and I desperately needed to lay down for a minute and gain some strength and relax a little so my chest would loosen up in order to breathe a little easier. I sat up in time to see another cop car pulling in and driving my way. I could not deal with trying to explain my situation to another cop, so I hopped into the driver's seat and drove away. Get the symbolism. I continued to run from 'the law' because I continued to run from YHVH'S Law - HIS Torah (teaching). Obviously, I made it back only by the Grace of YHVH. I eventually made it back home where I lived, and I would eventually make it to the rightful place with YHVH and Yeshua. And I would eventually stop running from YHVH's Perfect Law of Liberty.

When I got home, I laid down in bed, and was barely able to get out of that bed for what seemed to be weeks. I could barely make it to the bathroom to use the toilet and I can't even tell you how long I went without a shower. I was so nauseated that I could not eat. Not like I could have made myself anything to eat anyways. My bedroom just so happened to be all the way up a steep flight of steps that winded me when I was healthy so now I really could not afford the exertion of going up these stairs anymore than I had to. I had no strength at this point. My husband really did not like talking to me any longer. He did not understand why I just laid in bed and tried not to move. I was dying and nobody even seemed to care. My oldest 2 children now lived out of state and my parents were back in Florida where Abba had sent them, leaving me with no family or friends to help me. All of my other relatives lived 2 hours away or more as we moved away when I was 6 years old. This all happened this way because **'this thing was from YHVH'**. The wages of sin is death. What did I expect. I could not even talk on the phone, because I needed all the air I could get. I recall my daughter calling me one day, and the sadness in her voice as I told her I could not talk on the phone to her. She lived out of state and the phone was the only way we had to communicate. The anxiety seemed to exacerbate when I tried to talk on my phone because I had used that very cell phone device to send those dreaded 'images'- giving Hasatan free right to use my cell phone as part of my punishment. Hasatan knew every legal door I had opened to him and he was not about to let a single opportunity go to waste. All the while, I had no idea how to close a single door to him at the time. This was between me and Abba alone, and I needed to find out what Yeshua was showing me. I knew I could not live much longer without food. I ended up calling the squad 3 times in a span of a week. The last time I went into the hospital, I begged them not to send me home. I had several dreams that made it look like someone was trying to kill me. Someone I could not see. Well yeah, it was Hasatan himself trying to kill and destroy me and he was doing a real good job at it. The nurse in the ER asked me if I was suicidal. I told her no - that if anything, I was anxious and afraid I was going to die because of my dreams. I told her that Abba told me He was striking me with Anxiety for 3 years. She repeated me in a very condescending and mocking tone and looked at me as though I was a crazy person. Looking back, I suppose I was better off to keep most of this to myself. I kept asking her if she had a pastor there from the hospital chapel that I could speak to and pray with. I was hoping that maybe they would understand something that I didn't and help me somehow. Well at some point, a lady chaplain walked in to talk to me. Come to find out, she was of no help whatsoever. She confessed that she also struggled with severe anxiety and didn't know how to cope with hers either and told me at one point it got so bad that she begged and pleaded for YHVH to crash the airplane she was on that day so she could die. Who wants to be on a plane knowing a pastor could be sitting next to you petitioning to Almighty YHVH that He would crash the plane. I could not believe how many people confessed to me that they live with severe anxiety with no hope in sight. I did have hope. I just had a whole lot to learn before Yeshua was going to be able to take me through to deliverance. I first had to learn where I was going astray and repent and Teshuvah to turn back to the Ways of Almighty YHVH.

I became the laughing stock of the ER. It was obvious that my nurse went right over in a huddle with all the ER staff and was telling them all about what I had shared with her because they all turned and looked at me, laughed, and then turned back and continued in their huddle. Oh, I did not mention that I was in a bed in the hallway because they did not have any rooms available for me. A few bible verses come to mind of my humiliation all because of my sin and disobedience.

Ezekiel 5:14 I will make you a ruin and a disgrace among the nations around you, in the sight of all who pass by. 15 So you will be a reproach and a taunt, a warning and a horror to the nations around you, when I execute judgments against you in anger, wrath, and raging fury. I, the LORD, have spoken.

And also **Jeremiah 23:40** Amplified Bible **And I will bring an everlasting disgrace on you and a perpetual humiliation (shame) which will not be forgotten.**

Being my 3rd time in the ER in a week, they would not even start an IV this time. I desperately needed some fluids. I could not get them on my own. **'Sin will take us farther than we want to go, keep us longer than we want to stay, and cost us more than we want to pay'.** This quote by R. Zacharias is so true.

I continued to beg for IV fluids and they said they were going to send me home, because I refused to take the meds they wanted to give me. I told them I have really bad reactions to most meds and was begging them to just admit me with IV fluids - but they said they could not do that. No surprise that some lady from mental health showed up in my room and said she heard I was begging not to be sent home. She said there was only one option for me and that was if I would agree to go to mental health. Watch what you share with ER nurses. It may be held against you. I told her I was not crazy and didn't need mental health. She said it was my only option. I was so desperate to not be sent home, that I took her up on it.

I learned a lot while I was in mental health. I learned a nurse was stealing my meds and charting that I was taking them, when I was, in fact, refusing them. I was not about to walk around drooling with glassy eyes, slurring my speech, and not knowing what was going on. I also learned they had no real help at mental health and that much of the staff confessed they too suffered with anxiety and depression and this is why they worked there 'to try to understand it better'. I'm pretty sure we need to **get the log out of our own eye before we are able to see clearly enough to help someone get a speck out of their eye** Matthew 7:5 . These people were of no help whatsoever no matter how sincere they were in wanting to 'help'. They needed Yeshua's help for sure.. Not a bunch of medicine to mask their anxiety.

IF you are on anxiety medication I am not bashing you. And I am definitely not telling you to stop taking it. You may not be ready to stop taking it. IF you were to ever stop taking it, those instructions need to come straight from THE HEAVENLY FATHER. Only HE knows when you are ready to fully Teshuvah and close the doors to the 'spirits' of anxiety and depression. These are 'spirits' of anxiety and depression by the way.

They had nobody there to pray with us or offer Yeshua as help. Instead we had to color pictures, squeeze 'stress balls', go to their pointless group sessions (where I got to sit next to a boy that announced he had head lice during the middle of the session), and eat pig slop that could not possibly be good for any part of our health or mental wellbeing. I saw people of all ages. Even young, school age children. It was so eye opening and so very sad. And they offered absolutely no real, lasting help at all. Their only solution was to dope people up and send them home and tell them to color when they felt anxious. Coloring made me more anxious. I can't stand the nauseating smell of crayons. Hasatan is relentless and he is after our children like never before. I met several young people in there for attempted suicide.

But there is some good news out of this mental health stay. I was a nurse for 26 years and it would have been 'unethical' to preach the good news to these patients. But I was not there as a nurse - and as a patient I was going to tell as many people as would listen about Yeshua and Abba. I actually was given the floor to speak through several of our meetings. Luke 21:13 comes to mind: NLT **But this will be your opportunity to tell them about me.** Many hungry people asking me so many questions. Even the employee in charge of the group looked intently at me when someone else would ask me a question about the Word of Yehovah as if he himself seemed to have need of the same answers. As a matter of fact, upon my discharge this counselor discovered he shared my same date of birth. He told me *he knew there was some reason he really liked me.* Working out and releasing endorphins is supposed to help relieve anxiety and they did not offer as much as a treadmill up in this place.

I asked them a few times if there were any pastors or anyone that would pray with me. They did not offer any such services. This is preposterous. Don't they want these people to be set free. NO - Not when they seem to have a pretty good money making system set up already. People come in, get pumped full of meds with horrible side effects then they send them home just to expect them back in about 6 months when they build an immunity to their prescription drugs. They get read-mitted for the entire cycle to start all over again.

Since I was refusing to take my meds, and preaching and counseling their patients, I was soon discharged and sent home. When I got called into the Dr's room and she told me she was discharging me, I cried and begged to not be sent home to my husband who would exacerbate my anxiety con-stantly by yelling at me for laying in bed all day. I could no longer go out to eat with him and he did not know how to deal with any of this. Not to mention, we were having marital problems before the anxiety hit. This just made him hate me all the more.

I would spend the next several weeks just laying in bed strug-gling so hard to get my next breath. I could not imagine 3 years of this. I remember asking Abba Why my punishment was so much more severe than my offense. He told me He needed me to hate sin like He hates sin. It was working. I loathed myself for putting me in this mess. I had no idea about deliver-ance at this point. I was always taught that a child of The Most High YHVH could not have demons indwelling them. Well I learned they most certainly find open cracks in our armor and come in to wreak havoc until we figure out that we need to repent and teshuvah back to Abba's Ways.

CHAPTER 22

Yeshua began teaching me deliverance

Slowly, I was learning that I was not at all living for Yehovah and His Ways, but in every area I was aligned with the kingdom of darkness. I began repenting of everything that the Holy Spirit would show me. He had taught me that the 'holly days' we all grew up observing, were directly correlated to Hasatan and the kingdom of darkness. They had nothing at all to do with Abba and our Messiah Yeshua. Not once in YHVH's Word are we commanded to keep Yeshua's birthday annually. Unless, in fact, HIS birthday just so happens to fall during one of the Commanded feast days we are keeping already - but we are not told this information.. We are not even given a date as to when our Messiah was born. Not one person has ever concluded that Yeshua's Birthday was in the month of December. It saddens me greatly to know we are all teaching our children so wrong when all the while we think we are training them in the ways they should go. We as parents are unknowingly raising our children and grandchildren to serve Hasatan - the ways leading to death and destruction.

I was learning about keeping the Sabbath, that we were all told to NEVER keep. Why would we think we should morally keep the 'Ten Commandments', all except number 4. Abba even made sure He put it up in the top 5. Commandment in Hebrew is actually Mitzvah and means 'obligation'. If we say we want to be in Covenant with The Father, then we are 'obligated' to keep His Commands. Abba, Yeshua and all His Angels rested on the Sabbath long before He told us to rest with them. I believe They are still resting every Sabbath with us.

Jubilees 2:16 And He finished all his work on the sixth day -all that is in the heavens and on the earth, and in the seas and in the abysses, and in the light and in the darkness, and in everything.

17 And He gave us a great sign, the Shabbat day, that we should work six days, but keep Shabbat on the seventh day from all work.

18 And all the Angels of the presence, and all the Angels of sanctification, these two great classes -He has bidden us to keep the Shabbat with Him in heaven and on earth.

19 And He said to us: 'Behold, I will separate unto Myself a people from among all the peoples, and these shall keep the Shabbat day, and I will sanctify them unto Myself as My people, and will bless them; as I have sanctified the Shabbat day and do sanctify it unto Myself, even so will I bless them, and they shall be My people and I will be their Sovereign Ruler...

21 And thus He created therein a sign in accordance with which they should keep Shabbat with us on the seventh day, to eat and to drink, and to bless Him who has created all things as He has blessed and sanctified unto Himself a peculiar people above all peoples, and that they should keep Shabbat together with us...26 Wherefore do you command the children of Yisrael to observe this day that they may keep it kodesh (holier, set apart) and not do thereon any work, and not to defile it, as it is more kodesh (holier, set apart) than all other days.

28 And every one who observes it and keeps Shabbat thereon from all his work, will be kodesh (holier, set apart) and blessed throughout all days like unto us......30..on this we kept Shabbat in the heavens before it was made known to any flesh to keep Shabbat thereon on the earth.

32 And the Creator of all things blessed this day which HE had created for blessing and making it kodesh (holier, set apart) and splendid and glory above all days.

33 This Torah (instruction) and testimony was given to the children of Yisrael as a Torah (instruction) forever unto their generations.

Yeshua told us the Sabbath was made for man. Mark 2:27.

The writer of **Hebrews** tells us in chapter 4:9 There remains, then, a Sabbath rest for the people of God. 10 For whoever enters God's rest also rests from his own work, just as God did from His.

But everyone says it is only for the Jews and only for Israel. Are we not grafted into Israel through our Faith in yeshua (Romans 11:17). Galatians 3:7 said we are the seed of Abraham even though our natural bodies are not from Abraham. Know ye therefore that they which are of faith, the same are the children of Abraham.

Exodus 12:38 in the Amplified Bible says: A mixed multitude [of non-Israelites from foreign nations] **also went with them, along with both flocks and herds, a very large number of livestock.** And yet, it was this <u>mixed multitude</u> that Yehovah gave the Torah (or Instruction Manual) to.

Exodus 12:49 is clear that there is only 1 Law that is given to anyone who wants to serve Yehovah. NASB <u>**The same law shall apply to the native as to the stranger who resides among you.**</u> There are not 2 different Laws. And there should only be 1 bible, 1 body, 1 Messiah. Not 2 bodies, 2 Messiah's, and 2 different bibles - or 2 sets of Instruction Manuals. Or 2 sets of obligations we are required to keep. Yeshua is the Word. So there is 1 Word for all who draw near to serve Elohim. We are told over and over in His Word. **Leviticus 24:22 You are to have the same standard of law for the foreign resident and the native; for I am the LORD your God.** It can not be any more clear in **Numbers 15:15 The assembly is to have the same statute both for you and for the foreign resident; it is a permanent statute for the generations to come. <u>You and the foreigner shall be the same before the LORD.</u> 16 The same law and the same ordinance will apply both to you and to the foreigner residing with you.**

<u>**Ephesians 2:14**</u> **tells us that Yeshua Himself ...made <u>both groups into one</u> and broke down the barrier of the dividing wall, 15 by abolishing in His flesh the hostility, which is the 'Law composed of commandments' (traditions of men - not Yehovah's Commandments) expressed in ordinances, so that in Himself He might make the two <u>one new person</u>, in this way establishing peace: 16 and that He might reconcile them <u>both in one body</u> to Yehovah through the cross, by it having put to death the hostility.** The Word is very clear, and even Paul tells us there is no difference between male and female, Jew or Gentile, we are all **one** in Yeshua Messiah.

Galatians 3:28 NASB There is neither Jew nor Greek, there is neither slave nor free, there is neither male nor female; for you are all one in Yeshua Messiah.

We could not see these truths before because **we had inherited nothing but lies and falsehoods** Jeremiah 16:19. Hasatan is a deceiver. Let us never forget that. We must ask Abba to forgive us for believing the lies of man and not digging into His Word for ourselves to discover His Truth. Then we need to ask Him to remove the Evil Veil that Hasatan has put over our eyes in the Name of Yeshua.

I was even told I would be a heretic to keep Shabbat. I was learning about Abba's Feast Days- His Moedim that we are commanded to keep 'forever' as a perpetual statute. This is the '**assembling** together' we are commanded not to forsake.

I had always read in The Word where it says we have all inherited nothing but lies and falsehoods but I never thought this passage pertained to me and my family. Surely it was talking about only the Israelites who kept going astray. I never could have imagined it was talking about YHVH's entire congregation of children - Anyone who professes to be His Child. My parents and their parents didn't know any better either and both of my great grandfathers were pentecostal preachers. I in turn raised my children teaching them what I had been taught. Now that I had been reading the Word for myself, I began having a lot of questions about what I had been taught. But I figured I just really didn't understand Abba's Word as I would continually run into scriptures that conflicted my Spirit about what I thought to be True. I didn't know what to do with those scriptures. But surely the pastors behind the pulpit knew more than I did.

I began learning about these falsehoods and turning from them. Abba began teaching me about deliverance. But He was also teaching me that if I did not Teshuvah the demons could come back 7 times worse. **Matthew 12:45 NASB Then it goes and brings along with it seven other spirits more wicked than itself, and they come in and live there; and the last *condition* of that person becomes worse than the first. That is the way it will also be with this evil generation.**

Suddenly it seemed like the entire Bible applied to me and was written just because of me and my wayward behavior and I was now reaping the curses on disobedience just like The Word warns us about. My daily prayer was asking Abba to lead me and guide me into all truth and lead me and guide me out of every false belief system. I tell Abba, I do not care what the Truth is, I just want to *know what* The *Truth is*.

I had a lot of 'house cleaning' to do and needed to get rid of a whole lot of 'junk' that should have never been in my house to begin with. When I say house, I am talking about the actual home that I lived in as well as my bodily temple. The Word is very clear that we are not to have anything that belongs to the kingdom of darkness and the occult or we will become accursed like those objects. Deuteronomy 7:26 **NKJV Nor shall you bring an abomination into your house, lest you be doomed to destruction like it. You shall utterly detest it and utterly abhor it, for it *is* an accursed thing.**

Paul carried such an anointing on him of the 'Holy Spirit' that even aprons and handkerchiefs would pick up the Holy 'Spirit' as it touched Paul. Likewise, occult objects carry spirits too because they belong to Hasatan and his kingdom. So If you bring it into your home, just know there are evil spirits attached to these objects. And they will roam around your house and enter into you because you welcomed them with open arms by carrying them into your own home to begin with. This would include all your **decorations** for xmas, halloween, the bunny rabbit holly day (that people like to call Easter), Valentine's Day, etc. These are all items devoted to Hasatan and doomed to destruction.

So If you are still 'decking your halls with boughs of 'holly' - just know the demons are right there with you. Witches use 'holly' for their spells. Xmas is a pagan / witch's 'holly day'.

Acts 19 will explain what I am talking about regarding the Kingdom of Light. So it is likewise applicable for the kingdom of darkness. Except the Holy 'Spirit' from the Kingdom of Light always brings life, blessings, and healings, while the evil spirits from the kingdom of darkness always brings death, curses, and destruction. Verse **11 God did extraordinary miracles through the hands of Paul, 12 so that even handkerchiefs and aprons that had touched him were taken to the sick, and the diseases and evil spirits left them.**

This knowledge did not come to me overnight. My willingness to let go of most of my belongings did not happen overnight. But I will say, as you take the first step in going back The Father's Way and give up something for Him, each time it becomes easier and easier as your love for The Father grows and grows. Even though I had not arrived, I made a step in the right direction and knew I wanted to Teshuvah in every area of my life. Abba knew my heart and began allowing me to take myself through deliverance as I would clean up areas of my life and repent and Teshuvah - this is the method by which you shut doors to Hasatan and force the kingdom of darkness out. Before I knew it, the anxiety was much lessened and very manageable to the point I could now function in life. As I sit here and work on this book, I can say my anxiety is completely gone. **ALL GLORY BE TO YHVH AND THE LAMB FOREVER.** We serve a Good, Good Father and Mighty Powerful Savior.

Remember all those people who confided in me that they've struggled with anxiety and panic attacks all their lives and don't know how to get better. With man it is impossible to get better but through our Messiah, YHVH has made deliverance possible.

CHAPTER 23

Abba saved Jed just for me

My husband and I were driving through the parking lot on the way to get groceries when my cell phone rang. The lady on the other end was informing us that the boxer puppies my husband had enquired about were ready for adoption and they were actually at an RV place being adopted out as she spoke. My husband immediately headed in that direction to go get him a boxer puppy.

As we arrived, I saw all kinds of people inside the Rv building holding puppies and filling out paperwork. I finally found someone in charge and asked if there were any puppies left. The lady pointed to the last puppy left - a little white puppy with brown ears and black around his eyes like a raccoon. She gave me the leash and told me to see what I thought about him. I did not have a good feeling at all. I didn't want to give him back to the lady because I did not have a clear direction from YHVH, and I didn't want someone else to grab him up. I needed time to pray. The more I prayed, the more I could feel like it was not going to go well if I got him. And why was he the last puppy left and nobody seemed to want him.. After about an hour, my husband was done being patient. He told me it was up to me if we got the puppy. Abba then had me look around and showed me how all the puppies had been adopted out immediately and how this little puppy was the only one left. Abba then told me the same words he told me in another instance when I did not want to go in a certain direction. He said, 'I saved him just for you.' Well how could I not take him now. My Heavenly Father picked out a dog just for me, and made sure nobody adopted him before we could get there for our dog. I told the lady we would take him, knowing the Holy Spirit was showing me it would be a bumpy ride ahead.

My husband named him Jedi because he was a huge Star Wars fan. Later, Abba had me call him Jed, meaning 'beloved of YHVH' because The Heavenly Father is not a huge star wars fan. As I am typing this book, Jed is now a little over 4 years old. He is still a handful but I have actually grown to really love this handful of 'all boy'. It did not come easy either. It has only been recently that I could say this. I never could seem to bond with Jed for some reason. He is not a very lovable dog. And he loves to use me as a chew toy. He is not a mean dog at all, but his chewing really does hurt. Yes, present tense. He still loves to chew. I kept telling my son he'd grow out of this chewing stage. I anoint him everyday and have even done deliverance prayers against his chewing. When I was a little girl, I had a stuffed dog that looked a lot like Jed. I named this stuffed animal 'digger'. This was prophetic that I would have a white dog, and boy is he a 'digger'. He could probably dig an entire pond rather quickly if you let him. He has destroyed many a yard that is for sure. Without trying to talk negatively about Jed, I will just tell you some of the struggles to show you the symbolism only. On top of digging, this boy loves to chew - mostly likes to chew on me and whatever I am wearing at the moment. I used to see it as a negative thing, but if I really stop to think about the symbolism, I can usually come out smiling. I put blankets on our couches so I can wash them frequently and try to keep our home from smelling like a kennel. Out of our 4 big dogs, Jed is the only one that loves to tear these blankets off the couch onto the dirty floor using his teeth, which in turn, causes holes all through the blankets. I just look at the blankets on the couch and wonder if they are even doing their job at this point with all the holes. Abba shows me a lot through this dog He gave me. I can see myself a lot through Jed in his disobedient and rebellious behavior. So when I complain to Abba about all the holes, he tells me he is training me up to make everything that I touch 'holy' too. Every time I take yet another behavior problem of Jed's before YHVH, I walk away realizing I can see some of his same behaviors in myself. I do not like to chew on stuff or dig holes in yards (Just to clear that up). I am talking about his stubbornness and hard headedness in getting him to obey.

As Abba was showing me to get rid of all my xmas paraphernalia, I noticed an xmas sweater that had been left at my home that did not belong to me. I was in a dilemma. I did not want to be partaker in this xmas sweater by sending it back to its rightful owner, but I could not just destroy this sweater either knowing it did not belong to me, but I needed it out of my home. I knew I needed to contact the owner of this sweater and let them decide what to do with it. As I was praying about it, I threw it out into the hallway along with some other items I needed to pray about. I always kept our 4 big dogs blocked off with a baby gate so they never had access to this part of our home unless I opened the gate for them. So as I am praying about this sweater, I looked, and Jed had gotten through the gate and chewed up the sweater. Very supernatural answer to my prayer, because Jed never got through this gate. He was very content hanging on the other side of the gate with his buddies. So I was able to text this person and tell them the sweater needed to go into the trash because Jed had chewed it up. They seemed to be fine with it. Problem solved.

There have actually been multiple occasions that Abba has used Jed to chew up something that belonged to the kingdom of darkness. Those are his 'good boy' moments when I actually appreciate that he just destroyed something.

It is very biblical that Abba orders animals to do what he wants them to do. He ordered the animals to go into the Ark to Noah (**Genesis 7:9**), He ordered and prepared a great fish to swallow Jonah (**Jonah 1:17**), and He sent venomous serpents among the people to bite them (**Numbers 21:6**). As we can see Abba can clearly use a dog named Jed to carry out His Purposes - like chewing up and destroying occult items.

I thank Abba that He gave us Jed. I feel like someone else may have beat the tar out of this dog by now. Abba knew this too. I had strict instructions from Abba to not hit Jed from the very beginning. It doesn't work anyways when you hit Jed. The more you hit him, the more he comes back even harder at you. He turns a spankin' into a time to whoop me. He thinks I am playing and jumps on me and chews me all the more. And he is nearly 100 pounds. As it turns out, he is not a boxer, but part pit. What he is mixed with is anyone's guess. If you look up a pit mixed with Saint Bernard - and look for an all white dog with a Saint Bernard face - that is what Jed looks like. I love the 'Saint' part. Especially since Abba uses this dog to teach me a lot of lessons and to destroy occult items.

I will admit, I get so many comments about 'what a good looking dog.' he is. And one day soon, when I learn to straighten up and be quick to be obedient, I believe that is when Abba will cause Jed to straighten up and behave too. He is a constant reminder to me that I myself have a lot to work on.

Remember I told you The Holy Spirit warned me at the RV place where we went to pick up Jed, that it would not be an easy road with this dog. He is a very large dog, very playful with an abnormal amount of energy and has no idea how much he hurts people when he runs at them and jumps up on them to tackle them. The shock collar 'worked' very well. I did not have to shock him. He knew to stop as soon as he heard the noise or vibration. But he also knew when the collar was not on him and took full advantage of those moments. Once I learned of occult symbols, I realized the metal parts to the shocker were in the shape of a **hex**agon. So I threw them in the trash and am now using a water bottle, which works way better anyways. Praise YHVH.

Jed can really try a person's patience. I have given Hasatan lots of legal rights to me trying to deal with this dog. I really don't want to relive most of them. But one example was the day he ran into me running full speed ahead in a big yard as the other 3 dogs were chasing Jed. As I fell to the ground in slow motion, I thought I would end up crippled or even dead from this hit. He messed up my knees and shifted my entire left side backward. I have spent a lot of money on chiropractic visits trying to get my body back into proper alignment. I will say, I know exactly what I had done to give Hasatan legal right to me that day in order to carry out this wicked plot against me. I immediately repented for that sin as I lay there in complete misery.

Here's the symbolism to this incident: I had sinned and made a comment about someone that I had no business making and I did not repent 'and take it back' because I felt like I was right. So later on while we were at the campground my dog 'Webster' took a big ole dump in the yard. I went right out to clean it up so they did not step in it while playing - Webster being symbolic of Hasatan who is always spinning a **web** to catch us in. As I stepped into the 'invisible web' that Hasatan spun for me, I looked up just in time to see Jed running directly at me with the other 3 dogs hot on his trail. I knew Jed was going to pummel me at full speed ahead and I could not seem to move. It truly was as if I was caught in a web and disaster was about to strike.

Another time was when I broke my hand on him after he and my other male dog got into a fight. The Holy Spirit immediately told me to pray and speak in tongues. So instead of praying and speaking in tongues, I went right out and started beating his head and face trying to make Jed let go of my other dog's ear before he tore Webster's ear off. For some reason, I thought Abba would make an exception for this traumatic experience and that He would understand. But Abba does not compromise His Word or HIS Instructions. I had clear instructions (from the beginning) to not hit Jed and to speak in tongues for this instance. I was disobedient to both commands. I was not allowed to go to the Doctor to have my hand set, so I still have pain and problems to this day because of my direct disobedience to The Holy Spirit. That was not one of my finest moments for sure. The stories go on and on. But I could never give this big, goofy dog away. Abba saved Jed just for me. Thank you, Abba, for Jed. Yeshua has taught me a lot of painful, but valuable lessons using Jed.

CHAPTER 24

I ran right into Hasatan's web

I am going to share some more real life stories about me to show you how the spirit world works in the physical. Hasatan wants us to sin so he can get legal rights to us. **Genesis 4:7 NKJV If you do well, will you not be accepted. And if you do not do well, <u>sin</u> lies at the door. And its desire *is* for you, but you should rule over it.** The word for sin could be translated, 'sinful thing' - aka 'demon'. From Hebrew strong's 2403 - Chattah'ah. So these demons are always lurking around trying to trip us up so they can gain legal rights against us and gain access to us. But we must learn to master our sin problem so we will rule over the kingdom of darkness instead of the kingdom of darkness ruling over us.

So here is an example - 'Based on a True Story'...about my life:

My parents, my Aunt, and myself were instructed by Yehovah to pray 3 times, everyday, together. At 9am, 3pm, then a time of our choice for an evening prayer. My mom started the prayer, then me, then anyone else who felt led to pray after that.

We all lived in different homes so we would do a conference call. We would end up talking so much that we did not get around to praying until, sometimes, 45 mins after our time set by YHVH Himself. The Holy Spirit kept checking my spirit and I kept trying to suggest we pray but somehow the conversations just seemed to go on and on. So YHVH finally told me to tell my mom that I was to pray first. This prompting went on for several days as I kept trying to justify that it would be ok because we didn't get started 'too' late. I did not want to hurt my mom especially at that time, because she was really struggling thinking Abba did not want to use her for some reason. If I would have told her that Abba was telling me to pray first now, I felt that would push my mom over the edge with her insecurity. I just really did not want to hurt my mom any further so I remained silent and did not say anything as I allowed this to play out for several weeks. I was unknowingly choosing my mom over YHVH by remaining silent.

In the process of my blatant disobedience, YHVH, in all His Pity and Mercy, did instruct me to anoint my teeth and pray, 'Strengthen my teeth', about 3 times every day for about a week. I assumed He had me doing this because I hated going to the dentist and He was preventing my teeth from needing dental work. Well, He was preventing major dental work because He knew something was coming that I could not see.

Remember **Amos 3:7 NASB Certainly the Lord GOD does nothing Unless He reveals His secret plan To His servants the prophets.** So, likewise, He makes Hasatan warn us of his plans. One morning as I was going through my daily routine, I walked through about 3 or 4 spider webs with my face all within about an hour span. I knew something was up in the spirit world, but did not take out time to seek YHVH about this. –HUGE MISTAKE.

I decided I was going to go outside and run instead of running on the treadmill that morning. I headed out and had just decided to jog around our block a couple of times taking me about 1.4 miles. I rounded the second corner, going '**left**' onto **Rock**ford. Abba had repeatedly told me He was making me 'Ford tough'. Obviously 'Rock' would be Yeshua and going 'left' symbolically is not good. I was right around the area where I had returned some lady's dog that had gotten loose several days prior, because someone had left the 'gate' (portal) open. I obviously had an open portal due to my disobedience. I was listening to the bible through my earbuds. It was talking about **sending out the hornets** to pursue the enemy. Out of nowhere, it felt like something got in the way of my feet. It must have been some giant 'demon hornets' that I could not see with the natural eye. There was nothing I could seem to do to catch myself and it all happened in slow motion. I hit my knees, then my hands, and then my body, then my face. I hit my mouth so hard. As soon as I lifted my head, I saw blood pouring out of my mouth. It looked like I just got punched by Muhammad Ali. I immediately asked YHVH what I had done for Hasatan to be able to do this to me because we are promised **'blessings on obedience'** and **'curses on disobedience'**. One can clearly see that something like this is a curse - so the question remained - what did I do to give Hasatan access to do this to me. Praise YHVH, in the Mighty Name of Yeshua, that I had anointed my teeth 3 times a day for a week 'to strengthen my teeth'. I was now understanding why The Father had told me to do this. I was so overwhelmingly thankful that Abba had not allowed Hasatan to break my teeth out. I just had no idea yet, what caused my open portal to Hasatan. I hit my mouth so hard, it felt like my tooth broke all the way through my lip on the upper left side. It took an entire day to make it stop bleeding.

— I knew it had to do with praying because I 'hit my knees' really hard.

— we are supposed to 'hit our knees' in prayer.

— I could not put my finger on what I did. So instead of scraping any fingers, I scraped up my right thumb. Several months later, I still had the scars on my lip and thumb.

— I **'hurt'** my <u>mouth</u> so badly, because I refused to **speak 'up'** and tell my mom I had to start praying first. Hasatan, then, was able to slam my **mouth 'down'**. I was disobedient to Abba because I did not want to '**hurt'** my mom but chose to hurt Abba instead giving Hasatan the legal right to **hurt** me now. We have to realize that we are caring more about what our loved ones think more than what our Heavenly Father thinks when we choose their feelings over YHVH's feelings.

Yeshua tells us in Luke 14:26 NASB If anyone comes to Me and does not hate his own father, mother, wife, children, brothers, sisters, yes, and even his own life, he cannot be My disciple. The word hate really means we are to love everyone else less than our Yeshua and YHVH. We must put YHVH first and foremost in everything we do.

All the way home, I was begging Abba to reveal to me my sin, so I could repent and 'Teshuvah' - go completely back YHVH's Way. **Abba was completely silent** as I **prayed** and **called** out to Him - because I had 'kept silent' when The Father asked me to speak up on the **prayer call**. We are repaid according to our deeds. I walked home and got into the shower. Our Heavenly Father is so merciful. Even though He was silent for a moment, He always is so Faithful to show us our sins, so we can confess our sins to Him, so He will forgive us, and we can get those doors closed up, that we so ignorantly open to the devil and the kingdom of darkness. But in order to completely shut those doors we must Teshuvah and do what Abba instructs us to do. Not just saying we are sorry – but actually making it right. As I was in the shower the Holy Spirit revealed to me the legal right I had given to Hasatan.

I have learned that Abba wants us to target-focus and pin point our exact sin in order to close these doors to Hasatan. Why do we as humans not repent and Teshuvah, until Hasatan has wreaked havoc on us. Even after the devil showed me his plans that morning by repeatedly running my face into webs - I continued about my day, blindly, until I ran right into that intricate web that Hasatan set just for me.

We must be very specific on our sin. Abba already knows our sin. He needs us to see it, and confess it to Him and go back His Way. Yeshua was trying to show us this in **John 9:41**. They would not admit they were blind and needed healed. So Yeshua was saying, if they will not admit their sin, then He is not able to heal them.

I will prove a blanket repentance will not work. About 3-4 days in a row I kept singing and playing and asking Yehovah to accept it as my prayer to Him. The words in the song repeated **'Please Forgive Me'** over and over. I felt like I needed to pray this song, but I was not sure what my sin was exactly.

So even though I repeatedly asked YHVH to forgive me for any and all sins, knowing or unknowing, I could not be forgiven for this particular sin, until I did what Abba had asked me to do from the beginning. I was shown that I was about to 'face' a web that had been spun just for me, hence the spider webs I kept walking right through with my 'face'.

Here's some of the symbolism that I gave Hasatan legal rights to me on:

— I did not **'stop' and 'drop' everything and 'run' to my prayer closet** to seek YHVH's Face in Yeshua's Name when Hasatan was warning me - **so Hasatan 'stopped' my 'run' and 'dropped' me to my face on the cement.**

— I did not 'target' my sin and and go 'back' Abba's Way - **thus putting a 'target' on my 'back' to the kingdom of darkness**

— I 'ignored' Yehovah's command and remained 'silent' 'thinking' He'd understand that I did not want to 'hurt' my mom's 'feelings' - **so I walked all the way home as YHVH remained 'silent' and left me 'thinking' and wondering about what I had done. Hasatan was allowed to hurt me and cause all this pain I was now 'feeling' - and I felt like Abba was 'ignoring' me.**

— -'drug my feet' in doing what YHVH asked me to do - **so the demons 'drug my foot' on the sidewalk causing me to fall.**

— I was 'straight up' disobedient to The Father - **so instead of standing straight up, I found myself face to the ground - bowing before Hasatan.** The Word warns us we won't be able to stand before our enemies.

At that very moment, I had given Hasatan great pleasure that one of Abba's servants was now bowing to the ruler of darkness.

True repentance means you go back completely to the Ways of Yehovah and His Instructions.

CHAPTER 25

Tripped over Hasatan's obstacle

I had ordered some heavy duty portable fencing for our RV (a different RV that my husband and I had bought) -that had come in about 6 large, heavy boxes that my husband stacked against the wall at the foot of our basement.

I noticed the boxes had occult symbols all over them, but did not do anything when I noticed them. One Sabbath day, Abba told me to get a box cutter and cut those symbols off. I got the knife, went down to the boxes, then realized that the symbols were on EVERY SINGLE SIDE of all 6 heavy boxes. Thinking this was a test to see what I would do during the sabbath, I 'reasoned' that lifting these boxes would be too much work on Shabbat. **Jeremiah 17:22 says NASB You shall not bring a load out of your houses on the Sabbath day nor do any work, but keep the Sabbath day holy, just as I commanded your forefathers......Jubilees 50:8 says...whoever takes up any burden to carry it out of his tent or out of his house shall die.** The word of load or burden in Hebrew is 4853 - massa` and can also mean - **'lifting, bearing'**. What I do know is I gave Hasatan legal right to me on another Sabbath for lifting a heavy box to bring it inside off the porch. I can't recall what happened but whatever it was, the Holy Spirit showed me it was directly related to carrying that heavy load, not out of my house, but into my house. Hasatan does not mess around. If he can get a crevice in your armor, he is taking it quick, fast, and in a hurry before you know what hit you.

I was in a dilemma. I did not know if I was supposed to go against YHVH's written Word and if YHVH was even the one telling me to do this. I finally came at ease that the Father would allow me to do it as soon as Shabbat was over.

I laid the knife down there close by to remind me to do what The Father had asked me to do, but of course, I forgot and did not do it immediately after the Sabbath. I do recall thinking about it a handful of times but was busy doing other things at the moment and for some reason, I thought it would be ok to get to it when I had a more 'convenient' time. Which was never. The cardboard was very thick and I knew it would be difficult to cut and the boxes were very heavy to lift and maneuver in order to get to all of them. Quite honestly, I was walking to please my flesh instead of walking to please The Spirit - and Yehovah is Spirit. So I was not pleasing My Father because it is impossible to please YHVH in my flesh. As time went on, I began allowing my conscience to be seared with a hot iron and thought about this task less and less and kept putting it off. Our flesh will cause a lot of problems if we obey it. It actually will lead us to death if we do not learn to master it.

One day, as I put my phone in my pocket (the phone symboliz-ing my form of communication with Abba - because when He gave me Instructions, I may as well just put them in my pocket and ignored them) I stepped down a few steps on my way to the basement - then it was as if I tripped over something I could not see, I just fell straight down the steps and onto the basement floor landing on my right side which just happened to be the side I had put my phone causing worse pain to the situation. As I lay there half on my stomach and half on my side I immediately asked Abba what I had done to deserve this. Before I could even finish my sentence, I lifted my head just enough to find my face was just inches away from those boxes along the wall with my eyes looking straight into one of those occult symbols. I needed to 'look' no further than my own stubbornness of disobedience and procrastination. I knew exactly what I had done as this symbol may as well have been a neon sign flashing right in my face. Remember folks, obedience is better than sacrifice. Had I just been obedient dealing with those 'boxes', Hasatan would not have been able to trip me down the stairs over an invisible 'box' / obstacle.

Symbolism: Since I set Abba Instructions to the side - **I then unwittingly put my 'communication' device on my side.** Since I was being a **hyp**ocrite saying I loved The Master, but did not do what He said - **Hasatan was able to throw me on my hip.**

Since I did not want to 'face' the simple task that Abba had given me - **Hasatan, once again, brought me prostrate on the ground bowing to him- as I lay face to face with the 'marks of the beast' because I had chosen to set YHVH's**

command aside in order to follow hasatan's ways of disobedience, rebellion, and procrastination.

CHAPTER 26

PUNISHED FOR PROFANING YHVH'S SABBATH

A very close loved one who lived 2 hours away from me at the time, called me up and asked me if I could drive down to see them. This person was struggling with depression and really needed to spend some time with someone. I knew I would be needing to drive home on the Sabbath, <u>but at the time, I was not sure</u> in my spirit if taking a long journey on the sabbath was displeasing to Yehovah, especially to help someone who needed me. My mom had just recently made a 2 hour trip on a High Sabbath to go be with her elderly mom to help out her sister. I noticed that nothing had happened to my mom for making that 2 hour journey (at least not yet)- so I decided to do what was right in my own eyes, even though I felt a check in my spirit.

This person requested I bring their favorite dog of mine named Ginger. I soon headed out for what was supposed to be a 2 hour trip.

On my way, I got detoured **unnecessarily**. When I came off the detour – I realized I would not have even had to take the detour. **But I didn't know at the time** that I took myself way **out of the way**. I was just going by the road signs I saw. This trip supernaturally drug out for 4 hours instead of 2 hours. I had driven this before and it was clearly a 2 hour trip to this person's apartment. And then to make matters worse, my GPS took me to the wrong location. I knew there was a problem when my GPS said, 'you have arrived', when in fact it was in the middle of the street with not even so much as a driveway. I had not included 'Street' versus 'Drive' and of course the GPS chose the opposite of what I needed and as it turns out, I was now 23 minutes from their actual apartment.

By the time I arrived I had been driving a long 4 hours. Almost as soon as I arrived my husband began calling about when I was heading home to help him with the rest of the animals. I knew at this point I was going to have to cut this trip short and head home the next morning on the sabbath. I contemplated whether or not to wait until Shabbat was over, making it sometime after 8pm that evening. I was not sure I even wanted to make that long drive after dark. So I ended up driving home during the 7th day Sabbath (Saturday). In my poor decision to please my earthly husband over my Heavenly Husband and Father, I would soon learn that I would pay for this long journey. I also learned over time that my mom would also pay for her long journey she took on the High Sabbath.

After I sinned by taking that long journey on the Sabbath my oldest son decided he was taking a long journey and moving back to Texas. As you can imagine, my heart felt like it sunk to my feet. How could Abba allow my son to move so far away again after just leaving Texas since graduating college.

My mom told me that in a conversation she had with my eldest son, he kept telling her that he **'had to go back to Texas'**. But my dad had spoken with him and my son told my dad there was some girl there he was talking to. An old time friend he had kept in contact with when he left Texas the first time. So my dad kept saying that my son was going back to Texas **'because of some girl'**.

In prayer one day asking Abba why my son was leaving again and taking a **'long journey back to Texas'**, He reminded me of my sin of taking a long journey to see my friend on the sabbath, so Hasatan gained legal right to take my son on a long journey farther away from me again.

So it was true what he told my mom. **'He had to go back to Texas'** as part of my punishment. And indeed he was going back **'because of some girl'**... Just like my dad heard. But that girl was me.

Abba, please, forgive me in the Mighty Name of Yeshua. I am so sorry. Please, teach me Your Ways – that I may forever walk in them.

I love You, Abba. I love You Yeshua, my King.

CHAPTER 27

Occult symbols

Revelation 19:20 NASB ... he deceived <u>those who had received the 'mark of the beast'</u> and <u>those who worshiped his image</u>...

It was time Abba took me into yet another deception that I needed to learn about. Somewhere in this book, I make mention of my dad giving me an RV. Then I later had to sell the RV to fix up our home. With the leftover money we went out and bought a bunch of decorations to put throughout the house. We had a 4 story home, so we needed a lot of decor to fill the walls and the rooms because if you recall we sold everything at the flea market about 4 years prior to this and we had nothing.

Mistake number one was not praying why Abba had us sell everything at the flea market to begin with. It was to get these occult symbols out of our homes for our own good. Since I did not seek YHVH as to why we were told to sell our belongings,

I took it upon myself to replace them all without praying if this was YHVH's Will. I just assumed it was a test of obedience when He asked us to sell everything we had and start fresh.

I was all done decorating and had everything looking so nice 'in my own eyes'. But it was not at all pleasing to the Father. This was an expensive lesson to learn. I also learned Abba did not care about me throwing away money. He cared about my obedience to HIM ALONE. After I was all done finishing up the final touches to our home, I remembered the words that YHVH had told me. He said, **'The least amount of things you have in your home, the better off you will be.'** I did not know why Abba would tell me this and I just pondered His words.

I was sitting at the table one evening looking across the room at some wooden words I had hung on the wall. Everything I had bought had something to do with my faith and that I wanted to profess my love for the Father and Yeshua. **There is a way that seems right to a man (or woman), but its end is the way to death - Proverbs 14:12.** The Holy Spirit kept drawing my eyes to the words hanging on my wall. What could the Holy Spirit possibly find wrong with the words 'faith, hope, love, and prayer'. I thought they really looked nice and they represented my beliefs. Now my eyes are drawn to some curly cues on parts of the **cur**-**s**ive ('curse if') letters. Then Yeshua asked me, why I thought those curly cues were on these **curs**ive words. I said I had no idea. He told me to take them off the wall and look at the back of them. I finally saw that each word had three, unnecessary curly cues incorporated in the writing. And then I saw it. Each word had three 6's when you turned the decoration backward. Wouldn't that be just like Hasatan to hide something on the back of a good meaning word. So ridiculous. I took them down and threw them into the trash. Knowing the trash truck would destroy them to pieces. Now that I was on to this little trick, I started seeing the 'mark of the beast' everywhere I went, in every store. It was on everything. Listen to the word **curs**ive. Listen to what we are really saying, 'curse if'.

On a side note: I was at a birthday party one day and the little girl could not read the message on her birthday card. Her mom asked why she couldn't read it. The 6th grader proceeded to say, because they never taught her how to write with all those squiggly lines. I could not believe what I was hearing. I immediately texted another little girl who I had taken care of since 10 months old as her nurse, to see if her school had taught her cursive. She texted back, 'no'. I was appalled that the education system had dropped the ball on such an important part of everyday life. I would later come to learn that 'this thing was from YHVH' and He was trying to put a stop to these occult symbols and there are a lot of occult symbols in the English cursive alphabet.

I would like to warn us all to be careful what you fight hard to 'keep' or 'bring back' when it may just be the Heavenly Father trying to get it out to begin with. Just like all my decorations I replaced… Maybe we should have not fought so hard to put 'Christ' back into xmas. It has nothing to do with Yeshua and Abba was trying to help us remove His Son from that pagan holly day. But we, myself included, never asked The Father what His opinion was, as a lot of us went out of our way to say 'Merry 'Christmas' when there was such a big tado about forcing us into saying Merry xmas. If we had the mind of YHVH, we would have praised The Father for giving us victory in finally changing the name of that pagan holly day instead of insisting we keep Yeshua in that 'mixed up' festivity.

The cursive capital L is an occult symbol. Why do you think a woman, off an old tv sitcom, had a 'curs'ive L on every shirt she wore. It is absolutely no coincidence the L is on her left side right over her heart. When you say L it is pronounced 'el' which means 'god'. The lowercase cursive 'l' (el) and 'e' are also used in the occult. Notice that the symbols of 'name brand' clothing are generally placed over the heart area too. I want to make it perfectly clear that I have nothing against the founders of these companies and shows but am only pointing out what YHVH's children should be careful to come out of agreement with. We are called to be set apart and separate. We are in this world but not to be part of this world. Our heart is supposed to be totally devoted to our creator, Yehovah, and not to any other god or goddess.

Here is a quick article you can read about the slogan of a name brand and how the founder arrived at it getting it from a murderer right before his execution:

https://www.rd.com/article/nike-just-do-it-origin/

Here is a link discussing how this same founder arrived at the name for their company and how it was intentionally named directly after the 'goddess of Victory'. You will find it at towards the end of the article: https://www.news.com.au/finance/business/manufacturing/were-out-of-time-itll-have-to-do/news-story/13c243fd8d48a0ebc62eb5d765880dc9

So what other brands are causing YHVH's children to come into the agreement of darkness..

As a child of YHVH we are not to even mention the name of another god. How do you think Father feels watching us run around advertising these fake gods, goddesses, and occult symbols on all of our clothing, shoes, golf clubs, basketballs, purses, necklaces, and the list goes on and on and on. These faux god brands are very expensive to pay for their 'name' and there is also a high price to pay for sporting these names over our bodies. I was having all kinds of knee, foot, and hip issues while wearing these clothes devoted to hasatan because of the legal rights I opened to him. I see why they call them 'Name brands'. Their names and symbols are derived straight from the kingdom of darkness and 'branded' right into the clothing. The kingdom of darkness has been 'trying to make a name for themselves' ever since the tower of Babel project came to a screeching halt. **There is a high price to pay to follow Hasatan.** You better understand that. **Exodus 23:13** NKJV **And in all that I have said to you, be circumspect and make no mention of the name of other gods, nor let it be heard from your mouth.**

Deuteronomy 7:26 NASB **Nor shall you bring an abomination into your house, lest you be doomed to destruction like it. You shall utterly detest it and utterly abhor it, for it *is* an accursed thing.**

I had to repent and Teshuvah and ultimately throw out 95 percent of my wardrobe because I had decided to be in covenant with The One and ONLY True Yehovah.

We are to put on the helmet of salvation, and a miter that says 'Holy to YHVH'- not honor another god/ goddess, by plastering their name on our heads via a headband or ball cap. We are to gird our hearts with Truth, not wear occult symbols over our heart. We are to put on the breastplate of Righteousness, not prance around in a shirt that has the big fat letters of another god/ goddess over your entire chest. We are to shod our feet with the preparation of the gospel of peace, not 'slip' our feet into the **'sole'** of a shoe that represents the kingdom of darkness in any way. All the while bringing death to our **'souls'** for serving another god besides anyone other than YHVH. Whatever happened to following the **'footsteps'** of Messiah. Hasatan knows the bible and is very intentional in how he chooses to deceive us and defile us in order to pull us away from our called purpose.

1 Peter 2:21 For you have been called for this purpose, since Messiah also suffered for you, leaving you an example for you to <u>follow in His steps</u>.

Psalm 37:23 The steps of a man are established by YHVH,

And He delights in his way. Is The Father delighting in our way when we are advertising the kingdom of darkness with another god/ goddess or with the 'marks' of the beast plastered all over us.

Isaiah 52:7 NASB How beautiful upon the mountains Are the feet of him who brings good news, Who proclaims peace, Who brings glad tidings of good *things,* Who proclaims salvation, Who says to Zion, Your God reigns.

Exodus 20:3 ESV <u>You shall have no other gods before me.</u>

Sounds like pretty cut and dry instructions if you ask me.

Ask yourself the question and be honest with your answer: If you are dressed from head to toe in a brand that is representing Hasatan and his kingdom - Can The Heavenly Father look at you and see you are wanting to serve HIM ONLY with all your heart, soul, mind, and strength. Actions do speak louder than words. Could this give Yeshua right on judgment day to say to you depart from ME because you went a whoring after other gods. You had better answer this question honestly and with 100 percent accuracy. If you say you want to serve YHVH and HIM ONLY then you are going to be forced to make some changes in order to follow HIM and HIM only. We must stop confessing HIM with our lips while our hearts remain far away from HIM - in refusing to rid these other gods out of our lives. It does not **profit us to gain the whole world, but lose our own soul** in the process. Mark 8:36 NKJV

Joshua 24:15 ESV

And if it is evil in your eyes to serve the Lord, choose this day whom you will serve, whether the gods your fathers served... But as for me and my house, we will serve the Lord. We must choose this day whom we are going to serve. If it is YHVH, then serve HIM ONLY and stop looking like the rest of the World and choosing who they choose to serve.

1 Kings 18:21 NASB The Word asks us the question: **How long are you going to struggle with the two choices. If Yehovah is Elohim, follow Him; but if Baal, follow him.'**

Luke 4:8 Yeshua Himself reminded us **what 'is written,' 'Worship the Lord your God and serve Him only.'**

Once I resolved with all my heart, soul, mind, and strength that YHVH my Elohim is The ONLY One that I wanted to serve then I had to set my forehead as adamant stone in order to follow him. Ezekiel 3:9 NKJV **Like adamant stone, harder than flint, I have made your forehead.** That means I can no longer place any other god 'before him', 'beside him', 'after him', or anywhere 'near him'. Yehovah must come first in every area of our lives.

Exodus 34:14 NASB—**for you shall not worship any other god, because YHVH, whose name is Jealous, is a jealous God.**

By the way - Yeshua is the ONE Who told me to look up these name brands and how they arrived at their names and slogans because I hadn't a clue they were names of goddesses. So it must mean something to YHVH for HIM to bring it to my attention and want me to know this bit of information so I could have the chance to Teshuvah.

We must stop making Hasatan our master and stop obeying the devil's commands while we set Abba's Commands aside. This makes us weak and emaciated and this is exactly why Hasatan deceives and seduces us to be led astray to follow other gods - hence we are actually following satan in so doing. Now he becomes our ruler instead of us ruling over him. Yeshua came to destroy the works of the devil. We must do as our Yeshua taught us so the gates of hades will stop prevailing.

A lot of health issues vanished as I began departing with my wardrobe that brought glory to any other god but YHVH. It immediately began slamming these legal doors shut that I had opened to Satan. My knees and hips healed almost immediately. All my shoes had to go because they represented another god or goddess and contained occult symbols and the demons they carry with them brought much affliction upon my body from gaining legal rights to me. I had **unknowingly** made Hasatan my ruler. It did not matter that it was unknowingly. I still paid the price even though I did not know.

I am reminded of a vision I had. I saw myself out in my backyard picking up dog doo doo wearing my white 'Yoga' pants. Yoga ushers in the Kundalini spirit in hopes to open our 3rd eye. This is pure evil and we must stay away from yoga and anything associated with yoga. I saw literal holes all through my legs - but only over the areas that these 'yoga' pants covered. These were little portals I opened to the kingdom of darkness everytime I put these 'yoga' pants on. So if you have clothing that has been dedicated to the 'yoga' god / the spirit of kundalini - it is an item dedicated for destruction and we will become destroyed by these items. I know from experience.

I do not normally use the New Living Translation or the Message Bible, but allow me to share these 2 translations of the same verse:

Deuteronomy 7:26 New Living Translation

Do not bring any detestable objects into your home, for then you will be destroyed, just like them. You must utterly detest such things, for they are set apart for destruction.

Deuteronomy 7:26 The Message ' **And don't dare bring one of these abominations home or you'll end up just like it, burned up as a holy destruction. No: It is forbidden. Hate it. Abominate it. Destroy it and preserve God's holiness.'**

We must start preserving YHVH's Holiness and bringing Glory and Honor back to His Name - and we had better start taking EVERY WORD of our Instruction Manual seriously because that very Instruction Manual might just testify against us on judgment day.

Yeshua carefully took me to some websites to show me a lot of occult symbols that witches, wiccans, satanists, Luciferians, etc use in their spells. I say 'carefully' because one needs to be very careful opening these sorts of websites (portals). They have curses put on them for people who open them up. I can feel the sorcery on many of these 'portals'. You want to make sure Abba has called you to go on these websites before you start dabbling and just opening up any ole website. Abba has had me to quickly close out many websites when I would get a little ahead of Him and open something I should not have. Before I could get the site closed up I could literally feel the sorcery radiating from the screen. Which are, in fact, demons coming out of the computer on assignment against you for dabbling where you don't belong. I could not believe how many symbols we use on a daily basis that have been incorporated into our everyday English language. This is done intentionally. The Word warns us there is spiritual wickedness in high places. These people are put in very high positions to see to it that everything put out to the public is plastered with these wicked symbols. THE BEAST SYSTEM IS BEING IMPLEMENTED RIGHT UNDER OUR NOSES. AND WE ARE ALREADY ACCEPTING 'THE MARKS OF THE BEAST' ON EVERYTHING WE BUY. The hashtag mark is a demon sum-moning symbol. You know, the tic tac toe board, also known as the pound sign. Whatever you want to call it, it summons up demons. It also invokes the dead. It goes way back to before the flood when the fallen Angels taught men to sin.

Enoch 8:1 Moreover Azazyel taught men to make swords, knives, shields, breastplates, the fabrication of mirrors, and the workmanship of bracelets and ornaments, the use of paint, the beautifying of the eyebrows, the use of stones of every valuable and select kind, and of all sorts of dyes, so that the world became altered.

2. Impiety increased; fornication multiplied; and they transgressed and corrupted all their ways.

3. Amazarak taught all the sorcerers, and dividers of roots:

4. Armers taught the solution of sorcery;

5. Barkayal taught the observers of the stars;

6. Akibeel taught signs;

7. Tamiel taught astronomy;

8. And Asaradel taught the motion of the moon.

9. And men, being destroyed, cried out; and their voice reached to heaven.

So this would explain why I kept seeing visions of 'enormous' tic tac toe boards with a tack inside a square: because this symbol is a 'way bigger' deal than we can imagine and can actually bring pain upon us when we step into these areas that are dangerous.

You may want to rethink the social media platform that loves using hashtags with every phrase. I've even noticed churches who advertise on their signs outside -looking like the rest of the world in this trendy little fad . **2 Corinthians 6:16 What agreement does the temple of God have with idols. For we are the temple of the living God; just as God said,**

I WILL DWELL AMONG THEM AND WALK AMONG THEM;

AND I WILL BE THEIR GOD, AND THEY SHALL BE MY PEOPLE.

17 Therefore, COME OUT FROM THEIR MIDST AND BE SEPARATE, says the Lord.

AND DO NOT TOUCH WHAT IS UNCLEAN;

And I will welcome you.

18 And I will be a father to you,

And you shall be sons and daughters to Me,

Says the Lord Almighty.

I am not looking my nose down at anyone. The only reason I am writing all of this, is because I was guilty myself and Abba had to send Yeshua down to me to introduce HIS TRUE WORD to me. I was the imposter Bride and didn't even know I was following the imposter - satan himself. I was that bride that went a whoring after all other gods except The True Elohim. I was not part of the True Bride of Messiah who is 'without spot or wrinkle'.

Abba, please forgive us for our ignorance in the Mighty Name of Yeshua. Lead us and guide us into all Truth. No matter what the Truth is, just lead us out of every false and harmful way and separate us from the imposter bride. **Hosea 4:6 NKJV** _My people are destroyed for lack of knowledge._ **Because you have rejected knowledge, I also will reject you from being priest for Me; Because you have forgotten the law of your God, I also will forget your children.** This scripture is so true. Also check out the last sentence. We all quote the first part of this verse but frequently leave out '**because we have forgotten YHVH's law,** He will forget our children.'

How many have wayward children or know families that have unsaved children. Have we ever considered this is our 'curse from disobedience' to breaking covenant with Father and not keeping His Commandments. Answer this honestly. You do yourself no favors by lying to yourself, sticking your head in the sand, and thinking Abba must be talking about someone else. I did. Everytime I read the Word, I thought I was only reading about the Israelites of Old. I had no idea He was still talking about the majority of His children who have all gone rogue. And we don't even know it.

Abba took me through my house, AND CLOSET, a little at a time. The Holy Spirit would fix my eyes upon a certain decoration or piece of clothing. He would be completely silent, then eventually He would allow me to see the hidden symbol and sometimes the meaning of the symbol. I do not know the meaning of all the symbols. But I just know what some of the symbols look like and that the occult uses them. It was then up to me what I would do about each item as The Holy Spirit would bring them to my attention to show me they represented the kingdom of darkness. My walls and closet began getting very bare until eventually I had no decorations left in my home and hardly any shoes or clothes left. But I knew I wanted to show my love and 'devotion' to my Heavenly Father by getting rid of all marks that had to do with the kingdom of darkness. Not to mention, they open portals to your home for the demons to come right into your house. Remember Deuteronomy 7:26 NKJV **Nor shall you bring an abomination into your house, lest you be doomed to destruction like it. You shall utterly detest it and utterly abhor it, for it *is* an accursed thing.**

This would explain why I had a dream one night that a demon's face was coming right through my family room wall. Why was it my 'family' room in the dream. Because my entire family was sinning unawares and giving access for the demons to come join our entire family.

As I learned the symbols of the occult, I realized a lot of these symbols are right on your phone, your computer, clothes, cars, etc. We are forced to use them everyday. How many times are you prompted over the phone, to type in your 10 digit phone number *'followed by the pound sign'*. Aka hashtag. Or we are prompted to type in the last 4 digits of our social 'security' number followed by the demon summoning symbol. We are not at all safe and 'secure' summoning these demons every time we turn around.

So we've already established that our home decorations, bedding, curtains, clothing, everything includes occult symbols. Our automobiles even have them all throughout. Our tennis shoes are big with occult symbols. Abba is very symbolic. We walk with our feet, so Hasatan wants to defile our shoes so he can 'defile our walk'. Look at the bottom of your sole. Most are inundated with **hex**agons. Do you hear the word 'hex'. Nobody is trying to hide it from us. We just don't catch on too quickly. Did you catch the fact that the hex's are covering the sole's / souls. Hasatan is very intentional when he 'needs' us to come into agreement with his kingdom in order to put hexes / curses on our souls. The hashtag grid is very popular as well as the diamond pattern. I bought a pair of shoes that the bottom seemed to be ok until YHVH told me to use a magnifier to blow it up. This is when I saw tiny little hexagons over the entire shoe that was next to impossible to see with the naked eye. This seems next to impossible to make a mold that would imprint thousands of hexagons on the bottom of the shoe. Why would someone go to such lengths to create this mold if there was nothing to what I am saying. Why go to such extremes just to then hide these symbols by making them next to invisible if there was nothing to these symbols being placed into your shoes anyways. Ask The Father to open your eyes in the Name of Yeshua so you can see these Truths if there be anything in what I am telling you.

For months The Holy Spirit kept taking my eyes to a symbol on a very well known brand of shoes. I had no idea what the Holy Spirit was wanting me to see. Out of nowhere, I finally saw the hashtag in the symbol of this shoe that I always thought resembled a sideways 'A' instead. The sideways 'A' is actually the symbol for Hasatan's tongue. Now all I can see is the hidden hashtag symbol that the kingdom of darkness uses to summon up demons. And then people wonder why they are walking around with foot pain, knee pain, joint pain, arthritis, etc.

I do not believe it pleases Abba for HIS child to run around advertising another god or goddess or wearing the 'marks of the beast' EVER. Ask The Holy Spirit to show you personally and convict your heart if this is displeasing to The Father.

I will no longer wear most 'name brands' because their symbols are very, very close to occult symbols. Beside the fact that you are unable to find 100 percent material in the occult apparel anyways. I have yet to find any of their clothing that is 100 percent material. Notice I refuse to use the percent 'mark' because it is an ancient occult symbol that has been around for centuries that has been incorporated into our English punctuation. These brands are all a **'mixture'** of cotton, polyester, spandex, etc. The more materials they mix together in one garment the better - in order to symbolically turn us away from The 'Purity' and Oneness with YHVH and Yeshua - instead it leads us towards the mixed up darkness. So much 'mixture' when the bible says we are not to wear anything mixed. Deuteronomy 22:11 NKJV **You shall not wear a garment of different sorts/materials, *such as* wool and linen mixed together.** Our clothing is to be symbolic of Yeshua because we are clothed in Yeshua. **NASB For all of you who were baptized into Christ have 'clothed' yourselves with Christ.** Galatians 3:29. OUR MESSIAH IS OF NO MIXTURE EVER so why are we 'clothing ourselves' in our Messiah with a 'mixture' of materials that The Word prohibits. Hasatan 'mixes' our fabrics to defile us bringing us into agreement with 'mixture'. We must stop mixing the kingdom of Light with the kingdom of darkness. We cannot partake of both kingdoms. We must choose which kingdom we will represent and follow. We have gotten so far away from Abba's Ways it is not even funny.

I know a lot of people who would argue that our clothes do not need to be 100 percent with no mixture but look at

Deuteronomy 22: 9 **Do not plant your vineyard with two types of seed;** if you do, **the entire harvest will be defiled**—both the crop you plant and the fruit of your vineyard. **10 Do not plow with an ox and a donkey yoked together.** If Abba prohibits mixing 2 seeds together in your crop and HE prohibits mixing 2 kinds of animals to work together, you can clearly see how HE hates mixing anything because He is very symbolic and HE is of NO MIXTURE. So what we 'choose' to clothe ourselves in would be no different.. and satan knows this. We just don't seem to get it and are being deceived and destroyed for lack of knowledge as we continue to worship the beast's symbols. Revelation 19:20 NASB **... he deceived those who had received the 'mark of the beast' and those who worshiped his image...**

I've heard people argue, 'I don't worship the beast'. Good.. then get rid of his junk out of your house and closets and prove to YHVH you don't worship the beast or his images.

So Yehovah began showing me more and more occult symbols and brought to my attention how these symbols are inundating everything we buy. Why. Because Hasatan wants us to come into agreement and accept the 'marks of the beast' on everything we bring into our homes. This gives him legal right to come into our homes where his mark resides. The bible is clear we are not to take the mark of the beast. But if Hasatan can make us come into agreement now with accepting 'the mark of the beast', then this will empower him to deceive us in the future when Hasatan intends to fully roll out his beast system and require we all accept his mark. We must be very careful and diligent to guard YHVH's Word with all our heart, soul, mind, and strength. We must not think that Matthew 24:24 was written in vain. .... **so as to mislead, if possible, even the elect.** Let us never get so puffed up that we think we are above taking that fall and being deceived.

When 'The Beast system' is fully implemented it would be nearly impossible for a child of YHVH to keep His Commandments. It is already getting next to impossible to go to the store and buy anything that aligns with the Word of Almighty YHVH.

So How much harm can these symbols cause. Well, I don't know what all their symbols represent. But I do know that the hashtag is a 'demon summoning' symbol. So how many demons are we all summoning up from the pit of hell on a daily basis because of our ignorance. No matter what the symbol means, we can't escape the fact that it represents the kingdom of darkness - who just so happens to have a wicked agenda against all of humanity. Therefore if we bring them into our homes we become accursed like the object. Meaning demons are on these objects because they are 'the mark' of the beast, so that gives the demons legal right to us as well, because we are in agreement that hasatan is welcome in our homes with 'his objects'.

I will tell you another thing. Be careful using these symbols as passwords to your personal info like banking accounts and the like. I noticed one day, when the Holy Spirit brought it to my attention, that I had a 'dollar sign' (another occult symbol) in my online banking password, and some other symbols on my other accounts. YHVH Warned me it was time to change my passwords and come out of agreement with the kingdom of darkness. I slid my feet a while wondering what damage could possibly happen if anything. It was only a password... So I thought... and it sounded like way too much effort to change all of my passwords. The Holy Spirit finally got through to me and I sat down with my phone and computer and started '*trying*' to change my passwords. Don't you know, all hell came against me on this endeavor. My phone went completely black a couple of times. My phone froze up more times than I care to recall. My phone, at one point, started making a loud noise as if I was sending a fax or something. If I finally managed to get all the way through to change the password, the moment I hit 'change password' an 'error' message would pop up and tell me to try again later. You know this was Hasatan telling me to give up and try again later. Don't you know this is exactly what I did because the 'spirits' of frustration won that battle and made me give up. The demons have access to our computers because they have all the occult symbols plastered all over them. On our calculators, phones, and keyboards. They are all over our devices and computers. I became so frustrated after about an hour, or so, trying to change my passwords that I finally gave up without getting a single password changed. The Holy Spirit kept checking me and told me that I really needed to take heed and get them changed. I did not want to relive that frustration of what seemed like a lost cause. Everytime I attempted to change a password, the most annoying demons would take over my phone. I just did not want to deal with this anymore. It did not even seem fair. I did not sign up to have demons come in and rule the world. But I did sign up to come into a covenant with my Heavenly Father. That puts a target on my back, and Like my Abba tells me all the time, this spiritual warfare needs to become a way of life for HIS children from this point forward. We all must learn to battle the enemy in the spirit. They love to wear us down to make us give up... Just like I did. But I have a news flash.. Demons don't have to rule over us if we would keep Abba's Instruction E` Manuel. Then we would rule over them like The Father promised us.

Daniel 7:25 NASB And he will speak against the Most High **and wear down the saints** of the Highest One, and he will intend to make alterations in times and in law.

Why did I not think to immediately anoint my phone and bind those demons in Yeshua's Name. Because I was not taught spiritual warfare.

One day, as I was looking at my bank statement, I realized I had a lot of expensive charges on our account that were not our purchases. SOMEONE HAD HACKED OUR BANK ACCOUNT. I remembered immediately I still had that dollar symbol on my password that I was unable to get changed due to demonic forces so Satan gained legal right to my bank account. I went in and tried to change the password. Once again, these demons of frustration and obstruction got busy tormenting me. The Holy Spirit told me to go get my anointing oil and bind them so I could get in. (I renounce the phrase, 'it worked like a 'charm'. We need to really watch these little cliche phrases we are so accustomed to using. They came straight from the pit of hell. Just another deception to make us come into agreement with the kingdom of darkness and sorcery.)

Nevertheless, I bound the demons and was able to change my password. I would love to tell you that after binding these demons, that I was able to go in and change all my pass-words. I actually was able to change some more passwords, but found I was having to bind these demons about every minute or less. They have legal rights to our devices because of these occult symbols. Even a simple question 'mark', exclamation 'mark', quotation 'mark', the asterisks 'mark', and the list goes on.

Have you heard of the term Elites. Recall all the 'ites' in the bible: Levites, Jebusites, Gadites, Moabites, etc. The suffix 'ites' means 'connected with or belonging to'. (El means god). The so-called Elites or El- ites are saying they are 'connected to gods' and they have ensured that we are forced to use at least one occult symbol every time we create a password. They have messed with the password rules in order to force us to choose a satanic symbol in making up 'our own' passwords. The computer is programmed and will not allow your password to be accepted without using one of their nefarious symbols. This is the beast system being implemented right under our noses. We have got to wake up.

Once again, the demons were on assignment to frustrate and wear me down. Once again, I gave in and quit changing my passwords, because It was taking so very long for each password. And like I said, for no reason whatsoever, I would complete all the fields and hit submit and it would say, **'we are unable to process your request at this time - please try again later'**. One thing after another would happen during this process of attempting to change my passwords. It was **unbelievable** really.

I gave up once again with only having changed a few more passwords. Of course, I set that commandment to change my passwords aside, because I never wanted to deal with this madness again. But then I had to deal with hours of trying to get these hacked charges off my account. I gave Hasatan legal right to me by deliberately ignoring the Command of YHVH to change my passwords so I could come out of agreement with Hasatan's kingdom.

I am not proud of the fact that I allowed several weeks to pass before I was **forced** once again to deal with this mess. I would look at the passwords I had set aside every single day and kept choosing to ignore them. Surely Abba could see the struggles I was having to go through in order to change even one password. It is not that The Father does not understand our frustrations - He understands all too well that these are some of the means we open doors to Hasatan's kingdom and YHVH is only trying to help us by showing us what doors are even open to begin with and how Hasatan gets them open to us, and how we can close these doors.

So now I was experiencing major urinary tract infection symptoms. I could not figure out what legal right I had opened to the devil for him to give me a UTI - until I went online to login to my teladoc. This is when I discovered that my password symbol was from the occult, opening the door to myself for Hasatan to afflict my health. Of Course he had the legal right to afflict my bladder, because I was being 'incountanant' (incontinent) to my Heavenly Father by ignoring His Command in changing my passwords. I finally sat down and made myself work on these passwords for **hours** to get them out of agreement with the kingdom of darkness.

And since I 'drug my feet' on being obedient, Hasatan was allowed to 'drag his feet' on leaving my bladder alone and It took longer than normal to get this infection out of my bladder. We are always afflicted according to our own ways and deeds.

One more caution where the 'mark of the beast' is hidden in plain sight is using (3) 9's in a row. It is no different than (3) 6's in a row. It is merely turned 'upside down' just like the kingdom of darkness, and 'not so obvious'. It gives Hasatan legal right to you through this method of deceit. Satan does not come to us with devil horns holding up (3) 6's for all to recognize. He is the master of deceit and is very good at hiding his 'marks' from you in order to gain access into your life so he can wreak havoc.

I recently placed an online order for some clothes including a pair of 'cargo' shorts. I even paid over 64 dollars to ensure they would arrive in 2-3 days with no threat of them arriving on my Shabbat. As soon as I placed the order, I realized my cargo shorts contained (3) 9's in a row in the sku number. Once I saw it, it stuck out like a sore thumb. I immediately called the company to cancel the shorts off my order only to be told it was too late. I was probably speaking to Hasatan himself at this point, because he had legal right to his 'mark' and there is no way it was 'too late' to cancel my shorts off this order that had only been placed less than 5 minutes prior. RIDICULOUS LIES. There is nothing wrong with 'cargo' shorts per say. The problem was the sku number contained Hasatan's 'mark' and was now 'connected' to these shorts. I knew this would not turn out well because hasatan never leaves an opportunity go to waste. So the 4th and 5th day of the week (Wednesday and Thursday) came and went with no sign of my package. I made several calls to the facility to find out where my package was that cost so much money to 'ship' in order to receive it before the Sabbath. I even called and had them leave special directions that the package was NOT to be delivered on Saturday. By this point, I knew in my Spirit that I was going to receive this package on my Shabbat. AND I DID. I spent so much time repenting for this mistake in allowing satan to profane YHVH's Holy Sabbath. Since it was **'cargo'** shorts that was connected to the 'mark of the beast' - this gave satan legal right to my entire 'cargo shipment'. Thus it made no difference how much money I paid to have it arrive early in the week. Satan's 'mark' was clearly on these shorts and he had other plans for this 'cargo shipment' and fully intended to bring it on my Holy, set apart day to YHVH - The 7th day of the week.

I left the package sitting at the end of the driveway all day until Shabbat was over. 30 minutes before The Sabbath ended, I found myself wiping up feces that my dog drug into my house on her paw and spread it all over the place. Why...because hasatan never allows a legal right to go to waste.

That package, the one containing 'beast poop'- 'sat on my property' all day long. So at the end of the day, my dog **'Web**ster' squatted on the property and left dog (beast) poop, that my other dog stepped in and brought inside to 'mark' up the floor and couch. Hasatan is always catching us in his **'web** of deceit'.

Within a 3 day span we had 3 separate encounters with the (3) 9's in a row debacle.

My parents sold a camper and had to open a new bank account to have some money wire transferred into their bank account. So the banker told my parents it was as good as done and gave them the confirmation number and told them the money would be in their account within 2-4 hours. They told them it would be safe to hand the keys over to the buyers and send them on their way as they had a long trip ahead of them. They reassured them that they had never had an issue once everything had been approved and a confirmation number had been issued. Well my mom and I both knew something was not right but we did not know what it was.

So the camper was long gone, the new owners were well on their way home, and that evening the money was nowhere to be seen. In the process of the day my mom happened to look at her new bank account information and realized their new bank account started with (3) 9's in a row. This explains how Hasatan could prevent my parent's money from going through even though the bank was adamant that nothing would go wrong at this point. So my parents had to rush to the bank the next morning and insist that they close out this new bank account because it contained the 'mark of the beast'. As soon as the account was closed out and new bank account numbers given for the wire transfer, it went through at record speed.

My Aunt had made the same mistake as me and placed an order with an item that contained the (3) 9's pattern and she too paid to ensure her package would not arrive on shabbat. She felt convicted over this purchase and called to cancel her order the very next morning. They said they canceled it successfully and she would not be charged. Well Satan was not going to give up that easy when he had full legal right to his 'mark' inside this order. The package was not canceled, her credit card was charged, and it showed up on Shabbat. I ended up with iritis for over 'seeing' my Aunt as she placed her order because she is not computer savvy and had never placed an online order before. Iritis is inflammation of the iris in the 'eye'.

Very painful and 'blurs your vision'. Since I allowed the devil to 'blur my vision' by compromising and over-'seeing' my Aunt in placing her order, satan was able to 'blur my vision' in my right eye. People, beware of the many ways Hasatan can gain access to you through something as miniscule as a tiny little symbol. These symbols hold a lot of power behind them.

So would you buy something for nine dollars and 99 cents.... Just a thought...would you purchase something for six dollars and sixty six cents...the latter being the obvious 'mark of the beast'. The nine looks identical, just not so obvious - just like Hasatan.

I will remind you again: Revelation 19:20 NASB **... he deceived those who had received the 'mark of the beast' and those who worshiped his image...**

CHAPTER 28

Flying kleenex and paper towels

From time to time, I would have a vision of a kleenex flying through the room. Sometimes it would be a paper towel. I kept asking Abba what this meant. He would be silent for a very long time and not tell me what the meaning behind these visions meant. I would think of this from time to time and ponder what The Holy Spirit was showing me. Finally, as I began learning of occult symbols I came to the realization that they sneak these symbols onto our everyday items in an attempt to force us to come into agreement with Hasatan's 'mark of the beast' unawares. And in the process, it defiles us. One day, I noticed these marks were on the toilet paper we use. As a matter of fact, there is a story about the toilet paper I will share in a moment. I began taking notice of these symbols on the napkins at restaurants. What happened to the plain napkins they used to have. They now either have a faint occult pattern imprinted over the entire napkin, that you can barely see, or they have a colorful display of their business logo all over the napkin with the occult symbols incorporated into their designs. Either way, I got myself into big trouble wiping my mouth and blowing my nose on these napkins. Then I began to realize why I kept seeing them floating through the air in visions. The kleenex especially reminded me of a 'ghost' costume at halloween when I child throws a white bed sheet over themselves and goes out 'begging' for candy. Or when they put a kleenex over a sucker to make it look like a ghost. They are definitely on to something as most kleenex give demon spirits legal rights to accompany them because they contain the 'marks of the beast' on them. Most kleenex look plain as they can be. Until you look at the edges of a 2 ply. They are pressed together with a diamond pattern around the edges that is so small you can barely see it with the naked eye. Well, we are 'begging' for trouble when we continue to come into agreement and use the 'mark of the beast' to wipe with. Whether it be your nose, your mouth, your table, or your rear end.

So let me tell you what happened to me. Abba showed which brand of each item that did not have any occult symbols as He always promises a way of escape. So I have learned to carry my own little stash of toilet paper and paper towels everywhere I go. One evening we had gone over to a friend's house to visit. I headed off to the bathroom without my purse and did not notice until I was already done using the restroom that I did not have anything to wipe with. I did not know what to do at this point so I 'compromised' and went ahead and wiped using their toilet paper. Surely Abba would understand. IT DOESN'T MATTER - I opened a door to hasatan the moment I came into agreement with his marks, and I would pay for this mistake. I began cramping so bad that night. Back at our home, I ran to the bathroom and had horrible diarrhea. Which was incredibly unusual for me. But this diarrhea episode was so very painful. Without trying to be crude, I don't want to miss a chance to teach you. So as you can guess, the demons had legal right to my rear end the moment I decided it would be ok to use hasatan's 'haunted' toilet paper. The demons entered me and caused severe cramps and diarrhea. I sat on the toilet and repented and asked Abba to please forgive me in the Mighty Name of Yeshua. I had made a huge mistake and realized this now. Compromising is not an option when it comes to the kingdom of darkness. You give Hasatan an 'inch' he will try to become your 'ruler'. Abba told me to bind them and cast them out. My cramps and diarrhea stopped as quickly as they had hit me. All Glory be to YHVH and the Lamb forever. And of course there is the instance I compromised using the napkin at the restaurant because I did not have anything else. You will find that debacle in the next chapter.

I pray you can start to see how a bout of diarrhea can actually be demons inside of you causing all the cramps and discomfort - when we just seem to chalk it up as something we ate.

CHAPTER 29

Gothic diamondback snake

One night after laying down to go to sleep I found myself just laying there having trouble getting to sleep. I kept thinking Abba needed me to go to the closet and pray. But I was too lazy and just sleepy enough not to obey. Of course it feels like the 'spirit of anesthesia' comes over me every time I feel Abba would like me to get up and pray.

The next thing I know, I felt something enter my right nostril that tickled so bad it caused me to sneeze twice. I sneezed So hard that I felt as though I came up off the bed with the second sneeze. That sneeze went right into severe pain in my chest, neck, right shoulder, and upper back. It was horrific. I guess you could say it was nothing to sneeze at. Well, now I was forced to get out of my cozy little bed anyways. When will we learn that we can do it the easy way or we can choose the hard way. It is our choice. We suffer needlessly because of our unwilling flesh. I went to the bathroom and took out the Tums when I heard Yeshua tell me the tums would not work. I wanted to believe that He was not really telling me this because I was desperate, so I took 2 with not even the slightest relief. I went downstairs and drank some milk and I proceeded to lay back down only to realize that the pain was now horrendous. My husband got home from work about 1am. As I got up to let the dogs out of the bedroom to greet him, Yeshua told me to anoint myself and HE asked me if I had 15 mins to give HIM in the closet in prayer. So I went in and started repenting not even knowing what exactly I was repenting for. Because of my symptoms I could figure out that my heart was not right, but what I had done was unknown at this point. I began to pray for forgiveness of my heart not being right and being a 'stiff necked' person again. Abba asked me if I wanted to go to the hospital. My obvious response to that was a resounding NO. He told me to pray against it because that was Hasatan's plan against me. I immediately went into the Courts of Heaven and got a restraining order against that assignment until I would actually find out my sin. Abba told me to go back to bed and that He would take away my pain. As I lay back down in my bed I noticed the pain calmed down immediately and I fell right to sleep.

Going to the courts of Heaven, I was able to get a restraining order for a time, so I could seek The Father's Face and find out what Hasatan was accusing me of so that I could Teshuvah.

The Holy Spirit reminded me of the dream I had the night before about getting out of my lane because I was driving my car and not watching where I was going.

In the dream: **I was watching my car video screen to see where all the other traffic was at.** I almost crashed several times and realized how dangerous and careless I was driving by not looking with my own eyes the road I was traveling on.

Instead I was watching where everyone else was at and driving according to where they were at. In other words, I was paying attention to where everyone else was at in their walk and was trying to base my life according to where they were at in their life and not according to where Abba had already directed me to be in my life. In my dream, I finally came to my senses and stopped and decided I would never drive again by watching the video screen **to see where everyone else was at**, but that I would need to watch and focus on the actual road that Abba was setting in front of me. So be careful who you are watching on youtube or any other social media channel. Be led by The Holy Spirit.

Then I was reminded of a 2nd dream: I had a glass snake tank in my bedroom. I saw my tiger cat, **Rick,** which means (strong, hardy power) going inside the tank. I told my youngest son to get him out so he didn't get bit by this deadly **diamond back** snake. Since Rick had gone in and out several times in my dream, it dawned on me that even though my cat didn't get bit while in with the snake- that there had to be an **opening**, aka, **portal** because the **cat** could get in and out. This would mean the snake could definitely get in and out also because of this open portal. As I was standing at the bedroom door I saw the snake come out and slither across my bed. The Holy Spirit zoomed in at the snake to show me it had a gothic, black, fuzzy, arrow head, with white eyes. I yelled for my husband who I was really hoping would take heed to the seriousness of the situation. **(my Heavenly Husband wanted me to take heed to the seriousness of the symbols on these napkins)**

Back to real life: The night that something had gone into my nose was the day I had gone out to eat. Abba had made me well aware of what most occult symbols looked like. They are used everywhere and are on most items we purchase and bring into our home today. They even decorate cookies and cakes in our bakeries using these ancient occult symbols.

These symbols actually go all the way back to before the flood when the fallen Angels taught man sorcery amongst other abominations. After the flood, man copied these symbols off the rocks and out of caves that they had been engraved on and continued in their sorceries and continued on sinning against YHVH.

So at the restaurant I realized I had still forgotten to restock my stash of Paper towels and Kleenex that I carried around in my purse everywhere I went. I had actually gotten really lazy about this and had gone out to eat several times without packing my own. I kept hearing the Holy Spirit's Warning, 'You have worked so diligently to get rid of this occult stuff and now you are getting laxed and allowing this stuff to creep back in.'

I have found that most of the time, the napkins at the restaurants will have the occult diamond pattern on them. This is 2 or more diamonds side by side creating a pattern.

I continually ignored these checks in my spirit, **as I looked around and everyone else was using them and nothing was happening to them**. (I was watching what everyone else was doing and not relying on what Yeshua had taught me- kind of like my dream). Even my parents who knew better were using the napkins from the restaurants. I was sure I must have been all wrong about these symbols. I continually ignored the Holy Spirit's warning. Even after the Holy Spirit repeatedly reminded me what happened to me when I used the toilet paper containing occult symbols and how the kingdom of darkness gained access to me 'down there' where the symbols touched my skin.

Despite all these warnings, I kept using the diamond backed napkins at the restaurants. I am human and I felt like an idiot packing my own supplies when everyone else was able to use what the restaurant supplied. I WAS CERTAIN THAT I WAS THE ONLY ONE IN ALL THE WORLD THAT PACKED MY OWN NAPKINS. The biggest warning was when I was just about to blow my nose using the diamond backed napkins but I proceeded to use it despite the warning because I did not have anything else to use at this point, due to my negligence of restocking my purse. I was copying the rest of the world, instead of listening to Yeshua and His many warnings.

This is how the demon was able to enter my nose. In my one dream, Yeshua was telling me to stop watching all the other **vehicles/ people** around me and just pay attention to my own walk with Him. Any other way is reckless and puts me in great danger. Because to whom much is given much is required. Luke 12:48 NKJV But he who did not know, yet committed things deserving of stripes, shall be beaten with few. **For everyone to whom much is given, from him much will be required; <u>and to whom much has been committed, of him they will ask the more.</u>** I knew better and was expected to adhere to Abba's Instructions for my life and to stop coming into agreement with Hasatan's kingdom by accepting his marks.

To get a better idea of how dangerous these occult symbols are to us..pay close attention to my second dream where Yeshua equated the danger of the diamond symbols to a **diamond back snake.** In my dream there was an opening/ **portal** that my cat was sneaking in and out of, hence Yeshua was warning me that I had an open portal because I continued to compromise and use napkins YHVH had warned me not to use. Yeshua used a play on words to show me the diamond back snake had a [gothic, black, fuzzy, arrow head, with white eyes]. So even though I was seeing correctly with my spiritual 'white' eyes, I was following the 'black' kingdom of darkness instead of my Yeshua and allowing my thinking to become fuzzy of right and wrong. But He finally 'got' through my 'thick' 'head' (break gothic into 2 words and you can see (**got- thick**). - hence I have 'got' a 'thick' head.

CHAPTER 30

My quest to find Yeshua's birth date

Ecclesiastes 7:1 a good name is better than good oil, And the day of one's death is better than the day of one's birth.

After speaking to several people about whether to observe Dec 25th as Yeshua's birthdate, I decided to go on my own search. I cannot find in the Word where we are commanded to observe Yeshua's birth date. Nor could I find where Yeshua's birth date is known. I heard anything from Mar 27- Apr, to Aug 21, to Sept./ Oct during Sukkot. The latter being my guess.

But one thing that was consistent from every source, was that Yeshua was definitely not born in Dec and absolutely not born on Dec 25th. The closest someone came to Dec 25, did say it was highly unlikely though.

187

As I seeked Abba to lead me and guide me.. I kept hearing Him say 'I don't want anyone to know His birthdate, or I would have made it known, making the date clear.'

A lady friend I met through a prayer call said that she heard a well known pastor say Yeshua was born in Apr.

I've heard people explain that Yeshua was born on the 1st day of the Feast of Tabernacles and circumcised on the 8th day of it. (Shemini Atzeret) **Luke 2:21 And at the end of eight days, when he was circumcised, he was called Y'shua, the name given by the angel before he was conceived in the womb. (ESV)**

So as I was busy praying and seeking Yehovah about Yeshua's date of birth both of my parents had a dream the same exact night and they had no idea that I was seeking YHVH for answers about this topic.

This is my mom's dream that she had 12-27-20 in her own words: I had a little tiny baby that I was holding up to my breast to feed. It finally took my nipple but then let go of it. I don't think it drank any.

My interpretation: we are commanded to observe Abba's 'feast' days. This baby -representing Yeshua- did not 'feast' on breast milk. We are not commanded to observe a specific feast day for the birth of our Messiah. If Yeshua was born during Sukkot - we are not given this information. We are only commanded to observe 'Feast of Tabernacles' and told the exact days in which to observe it from year to year as a perpetual statute forever.

Now take her dream back to The Word and see what The Word -**Yeshua**- says about this scenario:

Luke 11:27 BSB **27** As Jesus was saying these things, a woman in the crowd raised her voice and said, **Blessed is the womb that bore You, and blessed are the breasts that 'nursed' You. 28** But He replied, <u>**Blessed rather are those who hear the word of God and obey it.**</u>

Yeshua clearly responds to this comment that we are to SHAMA. -'hear **and** obey' YHVH's Word. Which does not tell us to observe Yeshua's annual birthday but The Word is quite clear on what feast days we are to observe annually. Leviticus 23 is a good chapter to start learning about YHVH's Commanded Feast Days.

Here is my dad's dream in his own words that he had on the same night:

Dream 12/27/20

Judy and I were alone in a hospital room and she was in labor. The nurse had 'left' the room to get the Doctor and Judy had started to 'deliver'. It was 'breach', and I saw a 'leg come out' and all of a sudden the baby squirted out and 'disappeared' over the side of the bed. I 'looked all over trying to find' the baby , under the bed and all around. I finally found the 'baby in a basket' on a chair beside the bed. It was 'wrapped in a blanket' and I picked it up and held up to Judy for her to see. It was a handsome, tiny boy. 'End of dream'.

My interpretation of my dad's dream: I can pick out a few characteristics of the dream with the life of Yeshua.

— Yeshua 'left' his place in heaven to come be born on this earth - and he came to 'deliver' us

— we are 'breaching' our covenant with Abba by adding to HIS Word and observing days He never commanded us. (In a moment I will give you an instance in YHVH's Word that this is not acceptable in YHVH's Eyes to just make up our own feast days even if we do dedicate them to HIM).

— 'a leg came out' - we are commanded to come out on 3 foot festivals and travel to Jerusalem to celebrate these 3 festivals annually.

— The baby disappeared reminded me of the time Yeshua disappeared heading home from one of these foot festivals when they had gone to observe The Passover / The Feast of Unleavened Bread. His dad and mom after 'looking all over', finally found Yeshua teaching in a temple.

— Yeshua was born in a manger ('basket') and wrapped in a swaddling 'blanket'.

'End of Dream'- because although we see Yeshua's birth in the Bible, we are never commanded to make an annual feast out of it. It tells us of His glorious birth - then… **'End of Story'**. That's it.

So if you think it is harmless to observe whatever day you want to observe and for whatever reason - See what FATHER thinks about this in His very Word:

Exodus 32 NASB

The Golden Calf

1 Now when the people saw that Moses delayed to come down from the mountain, the people assembled around Aaron and said to him, 'Come, make us a god who will go before us; for this Moses, the man who brought us up from the land of Egypt—we do not know what happened to him.' **2** Aaron said to them, 'Tear off the gold rings which are in the ears of your wives, your sons, and your daughters, and bring *them* to me.' **3** So all the people tore off the gold rings which were in their ears and brought *them* to Aaron. **4** Then he took *the gold* from their hands, and fashioned it with an engraving tool and made it into a cast metal calf; and they said, 'This is your god, Israel, who brought you up from the land of Egypt.' **5** Now when Aaron saw *this,* he built an altar in front of it; and Aaron made a proclamation and said, **'Tomorrow _shall be a feast to the LORD'_. 6** So the next day they got up early and offered burnt offerings, and brought peace offerings; and the people sat down to eat and to drink, and got up to engage in lewd behavior.

7 Then the LORD spoke to Moses, 'Go down at once, for your people, whom you brought up from the land of Egypt, have behaved corruptly. **8 They have quickly turned aside from the way which I commanded them.** They have made for themselves a cast metal calf, and have worshiped it and have sacrificed to it and said, 'This is your god, Israel, who brought you up from the land of Egypt.' **9** Then the LORD said to Moses, 'I have seen this people, and behold, they are an obstinate people. **10** So now leave Me alone, that My anger may burn against them and that I may destroy them; and I will make you a great nation'......**35 Then the LORD struck the people *with a plague,* because of what they did** with the calf which Aaron had made.

Notice verse 5 where they **dedicated a feast <u>to Yehovah.</u>** But notice verse 8 where YHVH says how quickly they turned aside from His Commands. Remember Yeshua constantly reminded us **we are experts at setting aside the commandment of YHVH in order to keep our own traditions.** (Mark 7:9)

Then notice verse 35 that YHVH strikes the people with a plague, because of their sin. Can anyone say 'Covid 19', with all its variants: Delta, Alpha, Beta, Gamma, Omicron. Abba promises 'blessings on obedience'. But the entire World has gone rogue and is defiant in the Face of Almighty YHVH. We are warned of 'curses on disobedience'. Abba sets before us life and death and He asks us to choose life but so often we walk the way of death and curses.

Nowhere in the Word are we commanded to observe Yeshua's birthdate. Nor can anyone arrive at Yeshua's date of birth. So what are we doing making up man-made holly days, all the while we are neglecting to 'assemble' at YHVH's commanded Feast days. Then we make up one of our own holly days that copies the pagan days and try to dedicate it as a Feast to Yehovah. YHVH is not impressed. We all inherited this Xmas pagan day and it has become our **man-made Tradition** that we have substituted for YHVH's Commanded Feast Days. It was already established among the churches before we were born and we were all told we are celebrating the birth of our Savior. But as I said, Yehovah never tells us to observe Yeshua's Birth. As we can see from Exodus 32, Abba does not take kindly to us making up feast days and celebrating them even though we say it is dedicated to HIM.

Why would YHVH ever tell us to keep a date from the Gregorian calendar anyways. Dec 25 can be an entire month off of Abba's time calendar from year to year. This makes no sense what we have done and we had better be repenting and doing a Teshuvah right back to The Father's Ways.

Notice this list of so called gods that were said to be born Dec 25- and said to have been born of a virgin just like Yeshua I might add:

---

https://www.nairaland.com/4251378/list-gods-born-virgin-25th

HORUS

An Ethiopian-Sudanese God, born 25th Dec, by a Virgin around 3,000 YEARS before Jesus.

BUDDHA

A Nepal God, born 25th Dec, by a Virgin around 563 YEARS before Jesus

KRISHNA

An Indian God, born 25th Dec, by a Virgin around 900 YEARS before Jesus.

ZARATHUSTRA

An Iranian God, born 25th Dec, by a Virgin around 1,000 YEARS before Jesus

HERCULES

A Greek God, born 25th Dec, by a Virgin around 800 YEARS before Jesus.

MITHRA

A Persian God, born 25th Dec, by a Virgin- 600 YEARS before Jesus

---

DIONYSUS

A Greek God, born 25th Dec, by a Virgin around 500 YEARS before Jesus.

THAMMUZ

A Babylonian God, born 25th Dec, by a Virgin around 400 YEARS before Jesus.

HERMES

A Greek God, born 25th Dec, by a Virgin around 200 YEARS before Jesus.

ADONIS

A Phoenician God, born 25th Dec, by a Virgin around 200 YEARS before Jesus.

JESUS CHRIST

A Roman God born 25th Dec, by a Virgin around 1-30 AD

Notice that nobody has been able to even figure out the 'year' of our Yeshua's birth. There is a 29 year span of an educated guess going on. What makes us think they have cornered the market on the 'day' of His Birth. That is ludicrous.

So why would we throw The Savior of the World into the same category of 'all the other FALSE deities.

(Deuteronomy 12 BSB) **2 Destroy completely all the places where the nations you are dispossessing have served their gods—atop the high mountains, on the hills, and under every green tree. 3 Tear down their altars, smash their sacred pillars, burn up their Asherah poles, cut down the idols of their gods, and wipe out their names from every place. 4 You shall not worship the LORD your God in this way.**

Notice at the bottom of the list **'Jesus Christ'** is called a **'Roman God'**. Yeshua HaMashiach is not a 'Roman God'. He is the Son of Yehovah our Elohim. The Creator of the universe. Yeshua lived during the Roman rule, but He was by no means a 'Roman God'. Jesus comes from the GREEK word Iesous. And 'Christ' comes from the GREEK word Christos meaning 'anointed one'. The Greeks hated Yeshua and would not have considered HIM to be their 'anointed One'.

As the Holy Spirit started taking me through these word studies and taking Yeshua back to HIS Jewish background, I thought it best to address Yeshua / Yehoshua by His proper Name. If your name was Bob, would you like for someone to repeatedly call you Allen.

I stopped using the name Jesus when I saw the definition online that **Jesus** was 'supposedly' the Son of God and a really good prophet but that Jesus was also used as a 'curse word'. Yeshua is THE WORD and He brings no curse with HIM. We bring curses upon ourselves by our own disobedience to The Word.

CHAPTER 31

My GRANDMA'S DELIVERANCE

As I was sitting in our vehicle waiting for my husband to come out of some meeting, I saw a vision of 3-4 very vicious looking demons on a vertebrae with their hands on the bones ready to break them at any second. I said, 'That can not be good' - turns out this is my go to phrase after seeing a horrifying vision of demons.

I thought it was my husband's back I was looking at since he had been having back troubles. I always suspected that everything was about my husband and his sins were about to be punished. It took me a long time to realize Father sent Yeshua to me to show me 'my' sins that I needed delivered out of.

This is how I also know demons will lay dormant in their host until they are allowed to attack. I learned through much prayer, and counseling my grandma, that she had inherited an evil, demonic cloak from her bloodline. She had a brother who was in constant, excruciating pain, who eventually shot and killed himself. Upon his death, those evil entities, through bloodline rights, had to transfer to someone in the bloodline and my maternal grandma, who was his sister, was chosen. The demons lay dormant for 40 years in my grandma before they began to noticeably manifest in her life and then began wreaking havoc on her back causing excruciating pain. I was also 'programmed' to believe that bloodline and generational curses were preposterous and not a real thing. Was I even taught any truths. As it turns out – NO – I wasn't.

My grandma had been very active and spry for being in her late 80's. She was still driving and doing very well for herself until she started having trouble with her eyesight. Well the time had finally come for the demons to make their debut in my grandma. Out of nowhere, my grandma began breaking one vertebrae after another until she finally ended up in a nursing home. I knew it was not God's will to put her in a nursing home and I tried to tell everyone but nobody else knew what to do with her. It got to the place where my Aunt could no longer handle her by herself and my mom and I could not be of much help living over 2 hours away. My mom went up for a couple of weeks to help, but who knew how long it would be before grandma would pass on. Other than the broken bones, we had no reason to believe she would pass anytime soon.

Abba sent me to Van Wert a couple of times to talk with grandma and explain deliverance and we talked everyday over the phone. My grandma didn't understand what I was saying because she had been taught the same as I had been taught. Nor do I think she believed most of what I was saying but allowed me to talk since I was her granddaughter and did not want to hurt my feelings. She still believed and held fast to all the false religious traditions that Yeshua was bringing me out of. I cannot tell you how many times I heard my grandma say, 'I've lived this long and have never heard what you are talking about' — or 'I've lived this long, and it has been fine up until now.'

'Up until now' are the key words. Something was definitely happening now and there was no denying it. I told her that Acts 17:30 says **God is done winking at our ignorance** and He is **now commanding all people everywhere to repent.** Hosea 4:6 tells us NASB My people are destroyed for lack of knowledge. Since you have **rejected** knowledge, I also will reject you from being My priest. <u>**Since you have forgotten the Law of your God,**</u> I also will forget your children. [don't forget we are to be a kingdom of priests now in the order of Melchizedek]. Let those words sink in, 'Since you have forgotten the Law/Torah of your God'. The Word promises us 'Blessings on obedience' and warns us 'curses on disobedience'. **Deuteronomy 28** NASB Now it shall be, if you diligently obey the Lord your God, being **careful** to do **all His commandments** which I am commanding you today, that the Lord your God will put you high above all the nations of the earth. 2 And all these blessings will come to you and reach you **if** you obey the Lord your God. -But on the reverse side- **Deuteronomy 28:15 says:** But it shall come about, **if you do not obey** the Lord your God, to be **careful** to follow all His commandments and His statutes which I am commanding you today, that all these curses will come upon you and **overtake you.**

It was not long before Abba Instructed us to get her out of the nursing home. I had been teaching her about demons and how they get legal right to attach themselves to certain objects and how we should not have such items in our homes for the demons to gain access into our homes through.

I could tell she really didn't believe with her whole heart what I was saying. But she desperately wanted to come home, so she reluctantly agreed to allow us to get rid of some of her items that were displeasing to Yehovah. Abba said she could not come home until she did agree to get rid of her xmas, bunny rabbit, and halloween decorations. She did insist on keeping a few items that I really felt the Holy Spirit expressly showed me needed to go. Since I, myself, did not know why those items could not stay (I only knew they could not stay) I let it drop and just pondered the matter in my heart. My parents went up to help my Aunt dispose of the items and called me to ask about some questionable items and to pray and repent for bringing those occult objects into her home, then anoint her apartment after the items were gone. But, like I said, there were a few items my grandma insisted on keeping. There was a bird cage with a 'fake' bird inside that a family member had given to her. I told my mom (as the Holy Spirit let me know) that was the most important object for her to let go of. Birds are symbolic of demons. Not to mention, that was an **'imposter'** bird with no life in it trying to pose as a real, life breathing bird. Have you ever heard the song, 'Once like a bird 'in **prison**' I dwelt- [sounds a lot like a bird in a bird cage] No freedom from this sorrow I felt'. I heard The Holy Spirit whisper to me, 'ONE MORE NIGHT WITH THE DEMONS'. Since my grandma could not seem to believe me, Abba would allow an object lesson to show her she needed to come off this fake bird in a cage. We got a phone call in the middle of the night that the squad was on the way because my grandma was going into <u>**congestive heart failure**</u>. Abba told me Hasatan had legal right to her. He said her **heart** was not right spiritually because she was **failing** to get rid of the **congestion** in her home. She was more afraid of hurting her loved one's feelings than she was worried about hurting and angering The Heavenly Father. We must learn to get our priorities straight. That goes for all of us, not just my grandma. Just a few chapters back I made the same mistake of not wanting to hurt my mom over Abba.

Abba has a way to get through to us when no one else can. After the object lesson, my grandma told my mom to get the bird cage out of her house and she never wanted to see it again. She proceeded to tell my mom to get rid of everything that was displeasing to Yehovah.

A little time had gone by, and Abba had me go to Van Wert and visit grandma again. I realized it was so I could look around her apartment and see there was still so much more that she needed to part with. Even though grandma told us to get rid of any items that should not be there, the Holy Spirit wanted my grandma to depart with each item out of her own free will. Besides that, my grandma soon forgot about her CHF object lesson that caused a trip to the ER and was back to her old mindset that none of this made sense to her having never heard any of this in the 87 years she had been alive. We had gotten all the pagan holly day garb out of her home, but now we had to work on some other, not so obvious occult items with 'symbols'. I knew what the Holy Spirit was pointing out so I took a mental note of all she had and what was displeasing to Yehovah because these items represented the kingdom of darkness. I also discerned that my grandma was not quite ready to hear that she needed to part ways with yet more items that were in her home. I began praying that YHVH opened a door for us to tell grandma it was time to throw out some more items.

I happened to overhear that my grandma was suffering with her eyes and losing her eyesight rather rapidly. When she said she was down to only seeing 'shapes and symbols' now, I knew Abba had opened that door of opportunity I had asked Him to open in order to help my grandma. I could also see that Hasatan was afflicting her eyesight because she was becoming like her statues that were in her home. 'Having eyes but not able to see'.

There was a little boy and girl statue sitting on a see saw, and a duck cookie jar that was sitting on top of her fridge. These were not so obvious to me at the time as to why these were displeasing to YHVH. But He took me to **Deuteronomy 5:8 NASB 'You shall not make for yourself a 'carved image', or any likeness of what is in heaven above or on the earth beneath or in the water under the earth.** Then Abba took me to HIS WORD in **Psalm 115:4 Their idols are silver and gold,The work of human hands. 5 They have mouths, but they cannot speak; They have eyes, but they cannot see; 6 They have ears, but they cannot hear; They have noses, but they cannot smell; 7 They have hands, but they cannot feel; They have feet, but they cannot walk; They cannot make a sound with their throat. 8 <u>Those who make them will become like them, Everyone who trusts in them</u>.**

Then Yehovah, like He usually does with me, began asking me questions to make me really think before coming up with an appropriate answer.

— Who is the life giver - Yehovah.

— Who is the imposter who tries to '**pose'** *as the real thing* but actually **takes life**. -Hasatan

He caused me to see that these statues that sit there and hold the same **pose**, and ___do not contain life,___ but were instead **imposters** of a real life being that Abba had created. You know, **the ones we are warned not to make or have a carved image of.** These non-living statues that are supposed to mimic a real life breathing human, animal, or plant, etc fit Psalm 115 perfectly. Every line. So if statues are the fake imposters of the real thing, and Hasatan is a fake imposter, then why should we come into agreement with the kingdom of darkness who represents the dead and not the living. I choose the 'real deal' that was created by Yehovah and Yeshua. We all have so much fake, imposter 'trash' in our homes that is the dead, fake version of the real life creation. Hasatan has an agenda for every deception he pulls over our eyes. Don't be deceived, Hasatan knows YHVH's Word better than most pastors. Did you catch **Psalm 115:8 Those who make them will become like them, Everyone who trusts in them.**

If we come into agreement with all this fake, imposter stuff, *then we will become just like these fake statues*. *'Having eyes and not being able to see'. 'Having ears and not being able to hear'* what the Holy Spirit is saying. **Mark 8:18 Yeshua asked, 'HAVING EYES, DO YOU NOT SEE.. AND HAVING EARS, DO YOU NOT HEAR.. And do you not remember.'**

I don't know about you, but I am choosing to come out of alignment with Hasatan's insidious ways. I told you, he always has an agenda to lead each one of us into a spiritual death. After all, he is the 'life taker'.

So even after all my grandma had **seen with her eyes** and **heard with her ears**, and experienced with her own traumatic health issues, '***she could not remember'*** what Yeshua had taught her. She refused to let us get rid of the duck on her refrigerator because her youngest son had given it to her, and he had passed away unexpectedly a few years prior. I saw with my own eyes that my grandma had 'become just like' her statues. She had eyes and ears, but could not reason,hear, or remember what the Holy Spirit was saying - just like her statues.

I told her 2 things: I told her that her son was in heaven now knowing the truth about all these fake, non- living statues and that he would want her to get them out of her home.

I also shared with her the vision that I was seeing as we were all discussing this over the phone. I saw a duck floating in a pool of water inside somebody's body. Can you guess what happened that night. Yep. We received a call in the middle of the night again. The squad was on its way to pick up grandma again because she was going into '**congestive heart failure**'. Remember her **heart** was not right because she was **failing** to part ways with the **congestion** in her home. Hasatan gets legal right to us according to our own deeds. Romans 2:6 WHO WILL REPAY EACH PERSON ACCORDING TO HIS DEEDS:

This is why I 'saw' the duck floating in water inside a person. The duck was the cause of her sin and ducks like to float in water, so Hasatan added some water to my grandma's chest (since it was her heart that was not right). She kept choosing to walk after the kingdom of darkness, so Hasatan would wait until the middle of the night when it was really dark to wreak havoc on her.

I would like to acknowledge that we see some statues of cherubim and oxen, etc. in the building of the temples. I don't have all the answers. But I know what Yeshua was warning us to get rid of and why. I also watched the doors be closed to Hasatan as each one of us eliminated these items from our own homes. Hasatan's days are very short and he is not messing around. This is probably why Yeshua told me 'the least amount of items I have in my home the better off I would be'. All I can suggest is pray and ask The Father if these items are displeasing to HIM to have in your own home and be willing to Teshuvah if HE says certain items must go.

Yeshua finally got through to my grandma by allowing this object lesson a second time. She told my mom, while still in the hospital, to get rid of the duck and she never wanted to see it again. She also told my mom to get rid of everything that needed to go and not to even ask her anymore but just get rid of anything that is not allowed to stay.

For sake of time, I drew a short version for you of how Abba got hold of my grandma. There is much more to the story and it was a battle for sure. I can not go in detail that she got sent to a nursing home twice. After almost not getting her out the first time, they sent her back for round two. We almost did not get her out the 2nd time. At that point, our entire family was against the decision to pull her out of the nursing home but I had direct orders from Yehovah to get her out of there. It was nothing short of a divine Act of YHVH to get her out the second time. I did not go into how Abba required my grandma to go back in time to a 70 year old sin and that she had to call a person and ask them to forgive her of this sin. This is how Hasatan got legal right to her 'back' to begin with through this generational curse she inherited. She had an unconfessed sin 'back' in her past.

I did not go into detail of how after all these things and after she told my mom to get rid of everything that needed to go, she was still adamant to keep her mattress 'protector' that had the diamond pattern on it. She said she could sew lines through it or something. I could not make her give up items that she still wanted. Abba has pleasure in a cheerful giver and a **willing** 'giver upper'. She had to do this willingly and from her heart.

In order to get her out of the nursing home the 2nd time, we had to ship her 2 hours to my mom's house so we could take turns caring for her.

Our family members were completely against us helping my grandma and taking her through deliverance and it even caused some lashing out from some hostile family members that did not understand the Ways of YHVH. They demanded we leave her alone and let her die. But Abba still needed to deal with grandma on some issues and would not allow her to pass until they had been acknowledged by my grandma and repented for.

At the very end of my grandma's life I know Abba was getting hold of her. You could hear her repenting over and over as she just lay there on her back with both arms raised in the air praying almost constantly.

Right before Abba took grandma, He had me, my mom, and Aunt all stand over her and pray in agreement for her to be healed. Everybody but grandma was hoping YHVH would literally heal her and she'd be fine. HE did heal grandma — by taking her to Heaven to be with Him and Yeshua.

CHAPTER 32

THE SEAL OF LUCIFER

Another hair brain idea I had was to go with the trend of getting a tattoo. And even a dumber idea of getting it on my lower back - the one the world calls a 'tramp stamp'. Which, as it turns out, described me perfectly in the spirit world in my attempt to be a 'Christian'. I went a whoring after every god except the True Creator, Yehovah. I remember the day I got my tattoo. I knew my husband really wanted me to get this permanent stamp on my lower back. He had also talked me into getting my bellybutton pierced. I would not even consider either one of these options in my walk with Abba now. So as I am sitting there ready for the tattoo, I could have never imagined how bad the pain was going to be over my boney back. The moment she started, I unknowingly spoke a prophetic utterance. I said, '**It feels like someone is cutting my back open with a scalpel without being numbed.**' I had no idea those very words would come to fruition about 15 years later.

So without trying to take you all over the place out of sequence, I will tell you about my entire tattoo experience. It is currently the year 2022 as I am still writing this book. In 2011 The Heavenly Father began waking me up. About 5 years ago, He began teaching me about occult symbols and how they were incorporated into so much of our products, clothing, and furniture we buy and How demon spirits can accompany these symbols because they represent the kingdom of darkness. So Abba told me to look up the tribal part of my tattoo that extended 8 inches across my entire lower back from hip to hip. Yes, Hasatan was proud of himself the day I walked into my home with this permanent 'mark of the beast' on my back. As I looked online for the sign that matched my back, I was horrified, as I stopped on the symbol that matched mine. How did Hasatan trick me into getting a tattoo that was called '**THE SEAL OF LUCIFER**'. I was appalled, petrified, and sickened all at the same time. But it was too late. It was a permanent mark on my back now. How did Hasatan tricked me to get this nasty, 'mark of the beast' permanently marked into my 'flesh'. Surely Abba would understand. I got it when I had no idea how to serve my Creator. He would totally understand and protect me...right...or would HE... So I just went on. I briefly shot some ideas through my head of how much it would cost to have my tattoo removed all of which is not a promise for a complete removal. Plus, by now, Abba had taken me out of my nursing career and I knew my husband would never come off of 5000 dollars. So I immediately threw those options out the door. But as time passed, I was mentally tormented by having this seal of Lucifer on my back. By this time in my life, I was diligently trying to clean up every aspect of my life. I wanted no part of the kingdom of darkness but here I was sporting Lucifer's mark on my back everyday, everywhere I was, it was with me and I could not get away from it. Then I began understanding that demons had legal rights to these symbols. **Joshua 6:18 says NKJV And you, by all means abstain from the accursed things, lest you become accursed when you take of the accursed things, and make the camp of Israel a curse, and trouble it.** By this time, I was becoming very bothered by this tattoo on my back so I found some tattoo removal cream that I spent close to 500 dollars on that supposedly worked great. Not happy about the fact that I hid this purchase from my husband. Number one because of the cost. But more than the cost, I knew my husband really loved this tattoo on my back and did not want me to get rid of it. How was I ever going to tell him. As I continued in my sin of hiding this from my husband, I prayed Abba would open a door for me to tell him that I was trying to get rid of this wicked 'seal of Lucifer'. In the meantime, I was so excited for this cream to arrive as it had such wonderful reviews. As it turns out, I am fully convinced those reviews were fake. If anything, my tattoo got darker. If it was not bad enough that this awful tattoo was on my back, I was deceived once again, into spending 500.00 dollars on some worthless cream. After about 2 months of diligently applying this cream on my back 2 times every single day, I finally threw it in the trash. By this time my husband knew and he too agreed it was making my tattoo darker. I tried scrubbing my back using abrasive scrubs and putting lemon juice over the tattoo to try to fade it. Nothing came close to working even slightly to fade this disastrous mess on my back. So I decided I would start anointing this tattoo 3 times a day. I prayed and binded every foul spirit that had legal right to me because of this wicked tattoo. One night, something woke me up just for me to see a demon floating through my bedroom. The demons always manifest into certain shapes in order to warn me of their plans. **Amos 3:7 says NKJV Surely the Lord**

GOD does nothing, Unless He reveals His secret to His servants the prophets. Likewise, I have learned that Yehovah makes hasatan warn us and reveal his plans to us too. We just need to walk with greater discernment to pick up on these warnings. So I am looking at this demon and all I could see was what looked like legs coming out of it and flopping around. I was so confused by this. I had also had a dream that my husband was standing by a bathtub when all of a sudden, he fell really hard through the glass slider of the tub with only his butt inside the tub and his legs hanging out the side. It was just known in my dream that he really injured his back really badly. My husband can stand in for me and vice versa since we are now 'one flesh' in YHVH's eyes. Obviously the rear end falling into the shower would represent that it was something on the back side near the rump that needed cleansed.

I got up the next day and did not think much about what I had seen. I continued to anoint my tattoo 3 times every single day. About one week later, my alarm went off at 6am like usual. All I did was reach up to turn off the alarm when I heard a pop in my lower back. I felt a horrific pain and realized I could not move and that I was not getting out of bed. This was a fact. I immediately asked Abba what I had done to give hasatan legal right to do this to me because I had learned by now that we are promised 'blessings on obedience' and 'curses on disobedience'. This was definitely the complete opposite of a blessing. Abba was very silent, but kept reminding me my tattoo was back there giving hasatan legal right. Of Course it had to be a day when it had been snowing the night before and we were in a level 2 emergency. My husband and I were back to having marital problems and he just proceeded to hop in the shower and not even ask me if I was ok. He actually made some very rude comments to me and did not believe I could not really get out of bed. He got ready for work and left me lying there helpless in bed. I was forced to call my 70 year old parents to come and help me. Not being used to getting up this early, I knew I would have to wait a bit for them to get up and get to me. I remembered I had my chiropractor's cell number to the receptionist. I texted her and told her I was desperate and that I could not even move. This is also when Covid was running rampant and everyone was supposed to be distancing. She texted back after a bit and said they wanted to help me, but it would be a little bit later, because they had to go into the office and they'd come on their lunch break. I was just so thankful for that much. My parents finally arrived and I won't even go into the awful details of my mom trying to help me use the bathroom lying flat on my back and unable to move. So embarrassing, humbling, and horrifying all at the same time - FOR BOTH OF US. Once the chiropractor arrived with her help, she rolled me over just enough to start adjusting me using the activator. Needing some answers, I asked her where my back was out. As she pointed to the spot I asked her if it was anywhere near my tattoo. She proceeded to tell me that it was right under the tribal sign of my tattoo on my 'left' side. Left, (symbolically) is also bad. So now I knew Abba could no longer wink at this tattoo. It was, straight up, giving Satan legal right to my back now. It was the 'seal of Lucifer'. That part of my back belonged to the kingdom of darkness and it was nobody's fault but my own. And everytime I binded those demons and cast them out of my back - I was only caus-ing more harm without getting rid of the problem first. Those demons were happy to leave just long enough for them to go find 7 other demons more wicked than themselves to come back into my back. It gave satan ownership of that area of my back. No matter how many times I anointed it, and binded the demons, I was only making it worse until I would come to a full repentance, called 'Teshuvah'. This means going completely back Yehovah's Way. This would mean I had to get rid of this tattoo no matter what the cost in order to close this portal. I now understood my dream I had about having a huge open portal and the door was broken and had to be removed and replaced in order to close off the portal properly. **Matthew 12:45** tells us without taking proper measure for a demon to stay away, it will actually get worse for us if it is allowed to return. **NKJV 'Then he (the demon) goes and takes with him seven other spirits more wicked than himself, and they enter and dwell there; and <u>the last *state* of that man is worse than the first.</u> So shall it also be with this wicked generation.'** So everytime I would bind those demons, they would gladly leave for a moment because they knew they could go gather up even more demons and come right back as long as that tattoo remained on my back. Abba had to allow extreme measures before I would be willing to pay whatever the price to get rid of that tattoo. I was on a long road ahead to recovery, but I knew I had to put something in motion. As soon as I was able to at least sit up on the side of the bed, I began calling everyone I could find for tattoo removal. Everyone I called only did laser removal which would take at least a year and a half with about 14 or so visits spaced out for healing time - with no guarantee that they could completely remove my tattoo. I could take no chances to leave even a trace of the 'mark of the beast' on my back. I needed this door shut pronto. I could feel the pressure of the demons in my lower back now and realized that the pressure was an abundance of demons that each one kept leaving (when bound) and coming back with 7 more wicked than itself. I needed this tattoo gone, so I could bind these demons out of my back once and for all. I was willing to pay the money now, but I could not find a Dr that could promise complete removal. I just kept praying and calling, reaching out farther and farther to not so local doctors - but at this point, I was desperate. Praise Yehovah in Yeshua's Mighty Name my perseverance paid off. I finally got hold of a Dr that was willing to 'excise' (cut out) the tattoo. With it being during the Covid outbreak, I had my consultation over a zoom video. I showed The doctor my tattoo and told him it was the 'seal of Lucifer' and that it needed to go like yesterday. He said he completely understood and would need to see me in person to see how much of the tattoo he would be able to cut out. He said he would get the entire tribal seal off for sure, but was unable to remove the butterfly that was above that because my skin would not stretch that far. So He worked up the prices and I decided to go the cheapest route and not be put out during the process. I do not like anestesia put into my body anyways and I did not relish the idea of being rolled onto my stomach, while being out, with my back still healing from that massive ordeal I had just gone through. I could not take any chances. I didn't even ask the name of my doctor and did not find it out until I had scheduled my surgery and the paperwork was sent to me. The facility ended up being 2 hours away. I knew this was from Abba when I received my paperwork and saw all the symbolism. I will only give the Dr's first name so as to not give his identity away. But his first name was Jason, which means 'healer'. His last name meant light. The lady that set up my appointment was Rachel which means ewe, or female sheep. After all, it was the week of Passover that my surgery was scheduled. It was actually scheduled for March 30, the day right after the High Sabbath during the Feast of Unleavened Bread. What better time to remove the leaven from my back.

My Abba and Yeshua are so Awesome. The place of my surgery was on 'Ewing' St. in Lancaster. Which means 'walled city, healthy, and pure'. My procedure was called ' excision (exorcism) of tattoo (to cut the tattoo out).

I felt Yeshua warning me that Hasatan had set a plan to prevent my surgery. So I prayed and prayed for Abba to not allow Hasatan to carry out his insidious plan against me. I had a dream that Yeshua was in my kitchen, where Hasatan was 'cooking something up'. Yeshua had hasatan laying flat on his back on some 'cot' as Yeshua had 'caught' Satan and bound his hands and feet holding them down with his strong hands. Hasatan looked raging mad. It was just known, if he got loose, that he was going to kill me.

I finally made it. It was surgery day. I was so relieved and so scared at the same time. I had already gone under the radar and was not asked if I had gotten the Covid test for my surgery. I also was not forced to wear their face diaper (mask) while in their facility. My Dr had already approved for me not to wear one, so every time someone tried handing me a mask, I told them my Dr said I did not have to wear one.

As I am laying on my stomach in the Operating Room, the surgery begins. I had had a dream that the shots hurt and DID THEY EVER. Here is where the prophetic utterance came in. I do not like medication going into my body and I have bad reactions to a lot of meds. So that morning, standing in the kitchen, I prayed in the Name of Yeshua, that Abba would 'not allow that numbing to 'affect me'. I meant that it would not have an adverse reaction on me when it started absorbing into my body. Well my prayer was answered just like I prayed it and the numbing did not take 'affect on me' - I felt every-thing. To be fair, It probably helped a little bit, or I would have not been able to tolerate it honestly. I could tell you what was happening and where the scalpel was through the entire pro-cedure. Hasatan was able to take one last 'shot' at me while that nasty symbol was still attached to me. As the DR started cutting, I felt the excruciating pain. Just like I explained the day I got this tattoo. 'It felt like someone was slicing me open with a scalpel without being numb.' This is exactly what was happening to me about 15 years after I uttered those words. I was being sliced from hip to hip without being numb. I told the Dr It was very painful, so he gave me the maximum amount of numbing he could legally give me and it still did not work. I felt it all. I felt every stitch go in after the tattoo was cut out. But it was worth it all to get rid of the mark of Hasatan.

After my surgery, my Dr asked me if I wanted to see the tat-too. I looked at that seal of Lucifer and said the words, 'good riddance'. The moment I said good riddance, I burped out of nowhere. If you know anything about deliverance, you will know that spirits are **ruach** in Hebrew or **pneuma** in Greek meaning 'spirit, **wind, breath, air**'. So when demons exit, they come out as a burp or gas a lot of times. Was I immediately healed right there on the spot. No, and here is why. Abba is very symbolic so he only allows Hasatan to get legal rights to us according to our very sins. **Romans 2:6 NASB who WILL REPAY EACH PERSON ACCORDING TO HIS DEEDS.** Since I 'drug my feet' and left the tattoo on my back, even after learning it was the 'seal of Lucifer', Hasatan was allowed to 'drag his feet' on leaving my back completely. Each month got easier and better. But since I went over 2 years 'knowingly' walking around with the 'seal of Lucifer' on my back, my healing time is going to take a little longer also.

CHAPTER 33

Yoga and the Indian meal moth

I am no expert on Yoga, the Kundalini, chakras, or any of that but I do know what Abba Father shows me through His Son and my Savior Yeshua by the Power of the Holy Spirit. Here's what I learned… I was standing in my closet one day and happened to see a strange looking, very distinct, tiny moth on my closet wall. I did not think anything about it at first until I began seeing more and more of them, mostly in my closet or in my bedroom. So I called a pest control company to come and check further into what kind of moth this was and why it was in my home. Let's see what the Word has to say about moths. **Matthew 6:19 Do not store up for yourselves 'treasures on earth'** (like yoga pants), **where moth and rust destroy, and where thieves** (demons) **break in and steal.** So what was I storing in my home that Hasatan was able to send in the moths (demons) to destroy. I received quarterly treatments in my home from pest control at the time (which Abba is currently dealing with me on, due to the toxic

217

chemicals being sprayed into our homes) so I was unsure why and how these moths were not dying.

Watch for recurrent and 'out of the norm' instances and also just learn when the Holy Spirit is pointing something out. Stop brushing these occurrences off and chalking them up as mere coincidences. The Holy Spirit is always trying to deal with us, speak with us, and show us things if we would just 'pay attention'.

I caught one and put it into a plastic sandwich bag and gave it to the pest control specialist that was sent out to investigate. It came back as an **Indian Meal moth**. What was Yeshua sent to show me..

As I pondered this and wondered what it could possibly mean, I went on about my business after asking Abba to show me what it all meant. I knew He would be faithful to show me in His Perfect Timing. It did not happen overnight either.

In the meantime Abba was dealing with me on some other issues about the kingdom of darkness that was actually bring- ing curses upon my life. As I was attempting to rid my life of all darkness, my husband was having fits thinking I had turned into some crazy fanatic. He had made the comment one day that I could get rid of all my clothes as long as I never got rid of my black stretch pants. The moment he said that, the Holy Spirit checked my spirit and let me know that day was soon approaching -to see if I cared more about what Abba thought over what my earthly husband thought. I felt sick to my stomach because I knew that day would come now since my husband just gave me specific orders . My husband was constantly reminding me that I was not the same person he married. I realized this- but what was I supposed to do with all these Truths that The Holy Spirit was bringing to me showing me yet another area where I had been deceived into doing Satan's will all of my life. I could not continue in these areas once I was convinced of my error that I was in and could now clearly see it in YHVH's Word.

All I could do was take it one day at a time and trust Almighty YHVH that my husband would stay with me regardless of what my Heavenly Father asked me to do to serve Him. All the while, I could see my husband growing angrier and angrier and drifting farther apart from me every time I chose Abba's Will over my husband's desires. I could see the hate in his eyes towards me growing ever stronger each day and it hurt so much, but I had to keep following my Yeshua because I had finally realized that it was time to Follow YHVH and serve HIM ONLY and make Yeshua my only Master.

I had come way too far to turn back to the world now. Galatians 4:9 warns us from doing this very thing: NASB

But now that you have come **to know** God, or rather to be known by God, **how is it that you turn back again to the weak and worthless elementary principles,** to which you want to be enslaved all over again.

Pay close attention to 'rather to be **known** by God'. This is how Yeshua can tell you to depart from HIM because HE never **KNEW** you. And HE won't KNOW you if you are not following HIS footsteps that HE walked out for us to follow. Yeshua tells us plainly the only ones who get to be part of HIS family - Mark 3:35 NASB For **whoever does the will of God**, this is My brother, and sister, and mother.

It is time to stop believing all the lies we've been taught and start allowing The Holy Spirit to reason with us and write Yeshua -THE WORD - on our hearts. We must allow The Holy Spirit to renew our minds and show us THE WAY, THE TRUTH, and THE TRUE LIGHT - And stop looking to the imposter, Hasatan, the fake angel of light.

IT IS NOT ABOUT A 1 TIME ALTAR CALL OF 'saying' you want to *'GIVE YOUR LIFE TO THE LORD'.* It is a 'LIFETIME' of being FULLY DEVOTED every single day to your Yehovah through Yeshua Messiah and allowing The Power of The Holy Spirit to **REMOVE** ALL sin **OUT OF YOU** and consecrate you to The Father alone and make us into the image of our Messiah Yeshua. To make us **perfect as our Heavenly Father is Perfect** Matthew 5:48. Yeshua would not tell you to be perfect if this was impossible. All things are possible with Yehovah and we are now given The Holy Spirit to help us so we are without excuse.

I was done being duped by hasatan any longer. The Bible warns us we've inherited nothing but lies, and YHVH's Word is so True. Once you set your heart and mind to know the Truth, the Truth really does set you free. I was being set free in so many areas of my life and could see and feel the liberation in so many areas. Looking back on everything my Yeshua has taught me, I am in total and complete Awe of HIM.

So one day, I decided to move my stretch pants from my draw-ers to the shelves in my closet. When I took all the pants out of the drawer I saw a bunch of blackish round spots all over my drawers. I figured it was from my black stretch pants some-how bleeding onto my drawers. It was not a big deal because

I didn't need that drawer for anything else so I proceeded to stack them on the shelf in my closet. I continued to wear these black stretch pants almost everyday to try to please my earthly husband. It seemed to be the only thing left that I could possibly please him with (even though I was instructed by the Heavenly Father that I had to wear a shirt that covered my rear end when I wore these stretch pants) and I totally agreed this was the proper thing to do.

Before long Yeshua finally told me it was time to do away with my stretch pants for my Heavenly Father. I knew I had to be obedient but it sure did not make it any easier knowing my husband fully meant what he said the day he told me I was to never get rid of those stretch pants that he loved for me to wear. I had slowly started to transition over to wearing other pants other than stretch pants now and my husband very much let me know that he noticed. So as I started taking the stretch pants off the shelf to throw them out, I realized those same black round marks were now on my closet shelf and back wall behind the pants. I now realized these were portals to the kingdom of darkness because of these black pants but why. So I threw out all of my black stretch pants but kept my white and gray pair. I thought it was the 'black' color only that I had to get rid of because symbolically it repre- sented the kingdom of 'darkness'. Beside for that, since Abba has allowed me to see demons, I have noticed that demons love to find black objects to blend in with to hide from us when they realize they have been spotted by a human. So I moved my white and gray pair to a different shelf. In the meantime, I was still seeing those Indian Meal moths only in my closet and bedroom. Where did Hasatan have legal right to me and why could I not get rid of this pestilence. I knew we were supposed to experience 'blessings on obedience'.

One day when I went to wear a pair of my 'white' stretch pants I realized that the white pair had also caused those same spots to appear in yet another area of my closet that I had moved them to. How could 'white' leave behind black spots...I knew for sure now that these were not spots coming from the dye of the pants. They were portals that had been 'legally' opened in my closet to allow demons to flow through my home. I prayed a little more fervently for some answers because I knew there was more than I could see with my natural mind now. I recall a vision that I had also of my standing in my backyard wearing those white stretch pants and there were open holes all through my legs but only where the stretch pants were at. Now I knew these stretch pants were opening portals to me and this was the reason for the Indian Meal Moths in my closet swarming around my clothes. Then the Holy Spirit began revealing why these stretch pants were displeasing to HIM and giving Hasatan legal right to me and my home. These were 'yoga' pants and yoga originated in 'India'. Moths destroy - Hasatan gained access into my home the very day I decided to bring those 'yoga' pants into my home. Yoga is no different than eating from the tree of knowledge of good and evil in the 'center' of the garden to make one wise. Yoga is all about awakening the kundalini serpent coiling up through the 'center' of your body and ultimately opening your '3rd eye' in your forehead. That even sounds ridiculous to read these words back. But it is real. STAY AWAY FROM IT as a child of YHVH.

Read this short paragraph I found online about Kundalini yoga and I will allow them to explain it better than I can:

https://www.verywellfit.com ›
an-introduction-to-kundalini-yoga-3566821

What Is Kundalini Yoga - Verywell Fit

Apr 26, 2021 The Kundalini is untapped energy, coiled at the base of the spine. 1 This energy can be drawn up through the body, awakening each of the seven chakras. **Full enlightenment occurs** when this energy reaches the crown chakra at the top of the head. Kundalini energy is often represented as a snake coiled at the bottom of the spine.

This snake is an actual 'spirit of kundalini' and is very real. Lucifer came in the form of a serpent at the beginning of all this sin debacle- if you recall. The serpent is something you want to steer clear of, so beware of any yoga products. I have found it very difficult to search for running shorts, sports bras, stretch pants, etc. because they have all been devoted to 'yoga' -aka devoted to the kingdom of darkness - aka devoted to destruction.. Buyers BEWARE. The 'mark of the Beast' comes in many different forms. Most of which are not too obvious. Hasatan could not so easily deceive you if his ways were obvious.

As scales, veils, sorcery, etc begin falling from you, you will look back at those deceptions you just came out of and wonder how Hasatan duped us in the first place - as now they will become clear and obvious sins to us.

CHAPTER 34

Miraculous sell of our home

One morning in prayer, Abba said to put the house up for sale. Immediately I realized this was a decision my husband had to be in agreement with. Abba told me to text my husband at work and share with him what Abba had just told me. I was going to text the words, 'I think', but Abba said I was not to use those words because I 'knew' what Abba had told me.

So I texted my husband that Abba said to put the house up for sale. To my surprise, my husband responded back quickly and told me he had been feeling that for a while and told me to get hold of a realtor.

In prayer, YHVH had revealed to me to call a realtor whom we had spoken to months before but ended up deciding not to sell at that time.

Yehovah had given me a very exact number to list the house at and I knew this realtor would need to be on board with what Abba was telling me. I told her I was instructed by The Most High to list the house for 280,000. The realtor shared her concern that she really did not think the house would even get a showing at this price although she was willing to do it. She did ask me to keep praying about that number while she was scheduling pictures to be taken of the house. Abba did not change His Mind and I shared with my realtor a vision that Yeshua had given me of a 6 digit figure of 267,000 or 276,000 I just could not recall which one I had seen now.

I also had to let my realtor know that she could not work or show my home on the Sabbath and that we did not want any open houses. She was very kind and agreed to all of Abba's stipulations.

Just moments after our home went on the market I began receiving multiple texts wanting to see the home. I even got a text wanting to see the home that night in about 30 minutes from listing it but my husband had just come home early that day with an intestinal virus and didn't want to be bothered anymore that evening. We ended up with 8 showings that next day and 2 more the following day. After cleaning the house, I took the dogs to the camper to wait out 8 showings.

My husband came to the camper after work still having diarrhea, so I left him with the dogs to run to a little mini mart gas station to get us something to eat. I also had to run to Dollar General to get some batteries for the remote so my hubby could watch tv. As I was heading to Dollar General YHVH was telling me He could get someone to offer 300,000 for our home. When I got to the camper - my husband made the comment, 'what if someone offered us 300,000 for the house'. I told him what Abba had just revealed to me in the car about that exact figure.

We had a total of 3 offers that evening - 2 of them were 300,000 plus dollars - but I told her she could show the home to 2 appointments the next day. After cleaning the house so spotlessly from the first 8 showings, I was already tired of this tedious process and was not at all wanting to clean the house again. Abba had shared with me not to work too hard in my cleaning efforts because He had already sold the house. At the end of that day we quickly narrowed down the 3 offers to just 2 offers.

When the Realtor called that night with the 2 offers. she gave me the figures of the offers - I texted her and reminded her of the vision I had of the numbers 276,000 or 267,000. These ended up being the figures after the realtor fees and taxes were taken out of the two different offers. My realtor called me and said she had goosebumps and could not believe how this was turning out. She also told me the names of the potential buyers. I asked her why everyone had different last names seeing there were a total of 4 last names out of 2 couples. She said she didn't know.

So as I was praying and asking Abba what we should do - and to ultimately lead my husband into the final right decision. I did not want to aid and abet any couple that was just 'shacking up' and assist them in continuing in that sin by selling them my home. As I was praying - My realtor texted and said - by the way - the one couple who offered 300,000 wants you to know that even though they have 2 last names - that they are married. So there was our answer. Abba said he sold it to a 'small family' and after meeting the couple I understood that statement. The husband was not large and they had started a 'small family' with 2 'small' children, 4 and 5 years old.

So Abba not only got the house to show way over what the realtor recommended us to ask, YHVH got us 20,000 over that.

We now had to get past the inspection which ended up passing quickly with absolutely no issues. Praise YHVH because my realtor was a little concerned due to the strict rules that VA loans often accrued.

But there was still yet another hurdle to cross. None of the realtors thought our house would appraise high enough to get what the buyers had offered. I began praying that Abba send out HIS Holy Angel to come in place of our appraiser. I have no idea if our appraiser was a Holy Angel, but I do know YHVH had this appraiser appraise our home at 300,000 without thinking twice. We were all in complete awe of what The Heavenly Father was doing through the entire process of selling our home.

I was asking Abba the day before our appraisal if it would appraise for enough. Abba told me to look at the name of the appraiser and his company's name.

Mark Stoner was his name - **Yeshua is the Corner Stone.** It was very common for Abba to instruct the people to set up <u>stone markers</u> when Yehovah brought them a **victory.**

He was from **Recon Inc.** - my day of **'reckon ing'** [**reckoning**] had come for Abba to bless my obedience.

So my A-PRAIS-EL (appraisal) turned out to be

'A Praise (to) EL' - (El meaning God).

My realtor called me throughout the process just in Awe of how the Father was quickly removing one hurdle after the next on our behalf.

ALL PRAISES TO MY CREATOR, REDEEMER, DELIVERER, HEALER, AND THE GREAT I AM.

THE ONE WHO STILL WALKS ON WATER, MOVES MOUNTAINS, AND SENDS BLESSING UPON HIS CHILDREN TO CHASE THEM DOWN AND OVERTAKE THEM.

CHAPTER 35

Some ways Hasatan deceives us

I will try to explain some of the ways Hasatan has deceived the whole world into coming into agreement with his agenda in order to gain legal access to us so he can carry out his wicked plots, plans, schemes, and assignments against us. And we have bought into his lies, hook, line, and sinker.

Lawlessness

One deception is to make us believe we are no longer to keep Yehovah's Laws/ Torah, statutes, and judgments. Since Hasatan got us to live **lawless** to YHVH's Laws - he was able to bring complete **lawlessness** to this world. This is why we are now living in total **lawlessness**. We came into agreement with hasatan's lie that we should no longer keep Abba's Laws because Yeshua covered it all at the Cross. If we are not keeping Abba's Ways - whose ways are we keeping. I heard a pastor say 'If we are not a Law keeper, then we are a Law breaker'.

There is a way that seems right to a man, but the way ends in death Proverbs 14:12. It is only Abba's Ways that are right. If it is not YHVH'S Ways then it is, by default, Hasatan's ways which will always bring us death and destruction. That's what he does. Kill, steal, deceive, and destroy us.

Unisex clothing

Nobody knows what gender they are anymore because Hasatan tricked us into buying gender neutral clothing. The WORD very clearly says in **Deuteronomy 22:5 A woman shall not wear man's clothing, nor shall a man put on a woman's clothing; for whoever does these things is an <u>abomination</u> to the LORD your God.** You can go on vacation and pick up matching shirts for the whole family off the unisex table or you can go to a craft store and pick up a cheap unisex tshirt to put your own designs on. The shirt is not designated for a male or a female therefore it is wholly designated to Hasatan's kingdom and designated to destruction.

This is yet another deception we fell into without even knowing it. Because of unisex clothing we now have **crossdressers** and anything and everything goes. Nobody seems to be able to figure out what gender they are anymore. All because Hasatan was able to make us set aside YHVH's Laws in order to go after his own ways - that completely contradict THE WORD of ALMIGHTY YHVH. These 'gender neutral' clothes 'neutered' us from our true 'gender' we were born with - hasatan robbed us from our God given identity as male and female. It seems like a free for all without any care of what our

Creator says is evil and abominable and what will ultimately bring curses upon us, our families, and this earth.

Word Magic

How about the lyrics, **'<u>Man</u>, I feel like a <u>woman</u>'** - this is WORD MAGIC - I bind the words in this song in the Name of Yeshua.

Now we have people choosing whatever gender they '**feel** like' being. Now we have men **'feeling like'** women and using women's bathrooms and women who **'feel like'** men. We now have men dressing like women who want to compete in women's sports and end up pummeling all the other 'biological' women in the contest. There is so much word magic going on in this world. It is coming out of our 'tell a visions' -[televisions], out of our radios, out of our government. It is everywhere. A lot of cliches that we are so used to saying everyday are putting curses out into the atmosphere not knowing how powerful our words are.

— 'Oh you are **killing me**.'

— 'I will **just die**, if you don't go with me'

— 'You are scaring me **to death**'

— 'You will be scared **to death**' [this puts a word curse on someone else]

— 'Oh that **shocks** me'

231

— 'Oh **Good grief**' - (since when is 'grief' good)

The list goes on and on... and on. The Word tells us **there is power of life and death in the tongue - Proverbs 18:21**. So of course Hasatan has us speaking nothing but death over our lives and everyone else's lives.

Hashtag is a Demon summoning symbol

Birds are symbolic of demon spirits in the bible.

Social media puts in the symbol of a bird, and throws in the **hashtag 'mark** of the beast' which just so happens to be a demon summoning symbol.

So how many billions and trillions of demons are being summoned up daily just through these platforms. The hashtag is also called a pound sign, number sign, a tic tac toe board game.

'X' is the symbol of Nimrod, who was the originator of sun worship and founder of Babylon. Why do you think they put x's and o's in the tic tac toe board. O's being symbolic of open portals. They don't try to hide it from us as they flaunt the 'mark of the beast' right under our noses and deceive us into participating because we just don't know what the 'marks of the beast' are.

Babel turns into Babylon

Change up the spelling a little bit and nobody is any the wiser. Since Hasatan cannot seem to get over the tower of

Babel flop, He just keeps adding 'on' to it and now it is called 'Babylon' - [Babel - on]

And by the way, the city of 'On' (in Hebrew) or 'Heliopolis' (in Greek) is a city known for its sun worship of their sun god 'Ra' - or '**Amen**-Ra'.

— America has erected one of the tallest **'Towers'** in the World - Called '**ONE WORLD** Trade Center'. Remember Yehovah destroyed the **'tower'** of **Babel** when all the people spoke 'one' language and nothing was restricting them from carrying out their evil desires. Take notice of how our **'towers'** resemble the **'Obelisks'** of the sun worshipers. There are no coincidences folks. Hasatan is always up to something in the grand **'scheme'** of things.

Hasatan has also made us come into agreement with his lie that the **World** revolves around the **sun**. This is not at all what the Word of Almighty YHVH tells us. These people are sun worshipers so of course they want to bring their sun worship agenda into this world and make us agree that the world revolves around the **'sun'**. They sure can not allow everything we do revolve around 'THE SON' OF YEHOVAH. If Hasatan can **deceive us** about **'the entire World'** - then he gets legal right to **'deceive the entire World'** about whatever he wants. What a deceptive plot, plan, and **scheme**. Hasatan desperately desires us all to revolve around the 'S-U-N' and not the 'S-O-N'.

'Don't tread on me' sign with the serpent

Luke 10:19 KJV Behold, I give unto you <u>power to tread on serpents</u> and scorpions, and over all the power of the enemy: and nothing shall by any means hurt you.

Of course Hasatan wants this sign posted everywhere. He is counter acting YHVH's Word because he does not want believers to **'tread on him'** and crush his head and when we plaster this sign on our vehicles and clothing we are agreeing with Hasatan that the ole serpent of old should not be tread on.

Statutes or statues

-Since we do not care about keeping <u>Yehovah's</u> **statutes** and completely 'destroy' His Laws, Abba is allowing these <u>man-made</u> **statues** to be torn down and 'destroyed' too. And since we are living 'lawless' to Abba's Laws, we are now given over to live in complete 'lawlessness'. Things I never thought the government could get away with, they are getting away with and nobody seems to do a thing about it. Why - 'because this thing is from Yehovah'. We are getting what we deserve and paying according to our own ways that go against The Word of Yehovah. People burning down other people's businesses, destroying and ruining cities and the list goes on while the government and law enforcement seem to turn a blind eye to all of it. Well they are blind to everything because we have allowed Hasatan to make us blind to everything as YHVH's children. The spirits of Chaos and Ra have been unleashed. Ra being their 'sun' god. Why would anyone want to serve a god that operates with so much hate, chaos, and destruction.

Non edible verses edible

Since we did not see **fit** to keep Abba's dietary Laws and began eating things Abba calls **non- edible, detestable, abominable, and abhorrent** - Hasatan thus gains access to sneak **non edible** objects into our foods and supplements that are not **fit** for human consumption either. Our foods, vitamins, vaccines, etc contain metals, plastics, fetus tissue, etc. and things we humans have no business putting into our bodies. Since we are careless to YHVH's instructions concerning edible and non edible food, we have proven we don't really care what goes into our bodies at all. If we did care - we would go back to our instruction manual to see that our Father instructs us to **make a distinction between the unclean and the clean, and between the edible creature and (non edible) creature which is not to be eaten. Leviticus 11:47.**

Whose laws are you abidin' by

-since we love **'abidin'** by man's laws and not Abba's Commandments we have been handed over to a man - ['a' 'Biden'] we are now **abidin'** by his man made laws and mandates or else lose your jobs, income, rights to go eat in public or workout in public gyms, or the right to be treated at the hospital, etc (if you refused to get the Covid vaccine).

It kind of sounds similar to a passage in the Bible when warning us of the 'mark of the beast.' **Revelation 13:16 And the second beast required all people small and great, rich and poor, free and slave, to receive a mark on their right hand or on their forehead, 17 so that no one could buy or sell unless he had the mark— the name of the beast or the number of its name.** I once heard the historian William Federer say, 'It is like someone setting the back of your house on fire, then they run around to your front door and offer to sell you a fire extinguisher. You will be so desperate you will pay any amount of money for it and thank them for being there for you.'

Where did Covid 19 come from folks..

Venmo

What about **venmo** - Does anyone see **venom** in the word scramble game. We had a curse come over our finances when my husband put this app on our bank account. It truly was like our bank account [wallet] had holes in it and our money was just blowing away. **Haggai 1:6 ...and the one who earns, earns wages** *to put* **into a money bag full of holes......9** *You* **start an ambitious project, but behold,** *it comes* **to little; when you bring** *it* **home, I blow it** *away.* .. YHVH'S Word is True and does not lie. We bring curses upon our own heads when we dabble in the kingdom of darkness even if we are unaware that we are.

Satan/ santa

I already explained the whole Santa deception but notice what Saa and ta mean in Hebrew on my diagram below. We all know satan 'make us desolate' and 'lays us waste' by dividing and conquering then locks us up in his 'chamber'.

Satan

Sa n ta

H7582 H8372

saa /shaw-aw` Chamber

Lay waste guardroom

Desolate

Polka dots

Did you **'fall'** for the polka dot fad. The Word tells us The Father is sending Yeshua back for a bride **without spot or wrinkle** Ephesians 5:27 -So Hasatan wants us to bring all kinds of spotted articles into our homes and agree with Hasatan that we love these polka dotted spots all over our clothing and everything in our home. Now he has just gained access to us to defile us and fill us with all kinds of defilement to add to our spots and wrinkles and it is no wonder we are all looking all wrinkled and haggard before our time.

Ever say 'dagon it'

Allow the Holy Spirit to check you as you use phrases and cliches that you have no idea where they came from. You need to understand that Hasatan is always up to something when he starts catchy phrases that we all love to repeat and keep on repeating for years to come. We don't give a second thought to these very phrases that Satan uses to gain access to us. Like the phrase 'dagon it'.

1 Samuel 5:2-5 Then the Philistines took the ark of God and brought it to the house of <u>Dagon</u> and set it by Dagon. When the Ashdodites arose early the next morning, behold, Dagon had fallen on his face to the ground before the ark of the Lord. So they took Dagon and set him in his place again. But when

they arose early the next morning, behold, Dagon had fallen on his face to the ground before the ark of the Lord. And the head of Dagon and both the palms of his hands were cut off on the threshold; only the trunk of Dagon was left to him.

Judges 16:23 Now the lords of the Philistines assembled to offer a great sacrifice to <u>Dagon their god</u>, and to rejoice...

Dagon was the Father of Baal also. Exodus 23:13 NASB

Now concerning everything which I have said to you, be careful; and **do not mention the name of other gods, nor let *them* be heard from your mouth.**

I clearly hear and see the god of the philistines when I hear 'dagon it'.

So when the Holy Spirit throws a red flag up the next time you use some cliche`, ask the Holy Spirit what you are really saying and what kingdom are you really representing in that moment.

Beauty and the Beast

I used to love the movie 'Beauty and the Beast'. What a wonderful, endearing love story. Or is it. Hasatan does not just fly by the seat of his pants and not have a reason for what he does. He is very subtle and works through tv and movie screen 'portals' to carry out his insidious plans. This movie portrays a young girl and a 'beast' falling in love. I kept hearing the word 'beastiality'. It is a very cunning way to sear our consciences with a hot iron so before we know it, we see nothing wrong with this girl wanting to be with a beast. By the end of the movie we are rooting for the beast to 'win this girl over'. Can we see this evil plot that the

'Beast', Hasatan, is behind all of this so that he can 'win us over' when we come into agreement with his movies and start rooting for the kingdom of darkness. Hasatan wants to win all of our hearts over. Especially our children...Just like the young lady, Bell. [Bel, signifying **'lord' or 'master'**].

Each one of us must start praying for more spiritual discernment in these last days if we don't want to fall for Satan's schemes from here on out.

Who makes up this stuff

— I graduated in 1989 and the phrase, **'you are killing me Has'** was very popular. I had no idea that another name for satan is **Has**atan. I don't think I even need to explain what the problem with this cliche is.

— When my children were in high school, a popular phrase came out, **'shoot me in my face'**. Who thinks up this garbage. That comes straight from the pit of hell. Right exactly during the popularity of this ridiculous catch phrase, I had a lady I graduated with get shot in the face and killed in the line of duty. This isn't funny or cute folks.

Sneakers

— Look closely at what you buy, what you bring into your home, what you wear, and what you are coming into agreement with. Why do some people call tennis shoes 'sneakers'. Hasatan is the 'sneaky' one, not a child of YHVH. I refuse to buy shoes that intentionally suggest we want to 'walk' this life or 'run this race' as **sneaky** children of Yehovah.

Take notice how many products give hidden honor to the sun, moon, and stars in the name of the product or on the outside label and picture of the product. The bible clearly tells us to be careful of this very thing. We must come out of agreement with satan's tactics that he is using to kill, steal, and destroy us all with. Deuteronomy 4:19 NLT And when you look up into the sky and see the **sun, moon, and stars**—all the forces of heaven—**don't be seduced into worshiping them.** The LORD your God gave them to all the peoples of the earth.

The Shape of an 'L' on your forehead

When I was in school it was popular to put your hand over your forehead in the shape of an 'L' when you were calling someone a 'loser'. There is even a song using this sign language:

All Star by Smash Mouth

'She was looking kind of dumb

With her finger and her thumb

In the shape of an 'L' on her forehead'

Remember that you pronounce 'L' as (el) meaning god. So we are going around holding the sign of 'god' to our foreheads thinking we are calling someone a loser when we are ignorantly insinuating that we are gods.

We must stop imitating the rest of the world and all their little catch phrases and hand gestures, etc. Most of the time it is another deception of Hasatan to gain access to us.

CONCLUSION

This life is difficult and I am not trying to make it sound easy so don't feel frustrated if you think that I have arrived and you can't seem to. I have not arrived either and we all have to set our foreheads as **adamant** stone (harder than flint) and be wholly devoted to our Yehovah through our Messiah. If you are trying to Teshuvah and you are still feeling beat up, this is normal - you now have a target on your back and the kingdom of darkness hates when you find THE REAL TRUTH - YESHUA MESSIAH - and begin following HIM. Hasatan will come at you like never before but do not fear this because you can rule over him like YHVH intended all along. Yeshua already prophesied that the gates of hades will not prevail - so one day THE GATES OF HADES WILL NEVER PREVAIL AGAIN.

We are still human and need to fight against our flesh every single day because the flesh desires to get its way every time

I Thought It Was Normal

and will lead us down a path of destruction every single time without fail. That is why we need to be walking 'after the Spirit'. God is Spirit. So we must, at all times, be led by **HIS** SPIRIT and not **our** own flesh. So even though you will experience healings and victories in some areas of your life for repenting and going back YHVH's Ways - Hasatan will not give up trying to deceive you in every area of life in order to gain other access points to you and this can be very wearisome at times because you are in a fleshly body. Hasatan's job is to wear you down and make you give up and say it is not worth it to follow Yeshua . Do not allow satan to win this life-long battle. YOU CAN DO THIS. If you have a heart for Yehovah and HIM only, HE will see to it that The Holy Spirit shows you these hidden Truths about HIS TRUE WORD and will enable you to stand in these last days.

Allow the Holy Spirit to teach your hands to war. Once you decide you are following Yehovah and HIM only -spiritual warfare will become a way of life for you. As you begin to teshuvah you close doors to the kingdom of darkness and begin stripping Hasatan of ammunition against you and then he becomes the weak one and you will reign victorious over the devil through Yeshua Messiah.

243